The Southern Stars

# THE STARS

## A NEW WAY TO SEE THEM

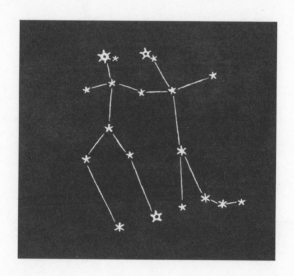

by

# H. A. REY

ENLARGED WORLD-WIDE EDITION

HOUGHTON MIFFLIN COMPANY, BOSTON

The planet positions on pages 134–135 are derived from *Solar and Planetary Longitudes* by William D. Stahlman and Owen Gingerich, University of Wisconsin Press, 1963. The full-sky triple-horizon charts on pages 74–105 are based on a copyrighted design developed by Charles A. Federer, Jr., for *Sky and Telescope* magazine, which has approved its use here.

*Eleventh Printing* H

ISBN: 0-395-08121-1

LIBRARY OF CONGRESS CATALOG CARD NUMBER: 60–13609

PRINTED IN THE U.S.A.

THE space age is upon us. Rockets are leaving our globe at speeds unheard of only a few years ago, to orbit earth, moon, and sun. Man has visited the moon, we have sent space probes to Venus and Mars, and words like "orbit" and "satellite" are picked up by children in the nursery.

And how has all this affected the age-old pleasure of watching the starry sky? Has it made stargazing obsolete?

It has not, and it never will. For we live on this earth and always shall. After the day is gone we shall go out, breathe deeply, and look up—and there the stars will be, unchanged, unchangeable. Even from the moon or Mars, or from Pluto, the outermost planet, the stars look the same as they do from the earth.

Night after night they are there. And night after night they arouse our curiosity, our urge for knowledge.

Stone age or space age, man will be asking the question his grandparents have asked before him and his grandchildren will ask after him: "What star is that?"

# CONTENTS

# PART I

# SHAPES IN THE SKY

# PART ONE

# SHAPES IN THE SKY

THIS BOOK is meant for people who want to know just enough about the stars to be able to go out at night and find the major constellations, for the mere pleasure of it.

Of course one can enjoy the stars without knowing them. But if you know them at least a little the pleasure is infinitely greater. It is fun to watch them announce the seasons, to see them rise at the expected times and places and follow their paths year in, year out, more reliable than anything else.

Besides, if you know the stars you are not easily lost. They tell you the time and direction on land, on sea, and in the air, and this can be valuable on many occasions.

And should you venture into outer space, anywhere in the solar system, where no earthly landmarks exist, the constellations would be your only guideposts, and familiar ones, too.

In short, to be familiar with the stars is both enjoyable and useful, and most of us would like to know them. The trouble is, few of us do.

This is odd. We do not look at the atlas often but we have no difficulty pointing out the fifty states. We can see the stars any clear night, ready to be studied and a challenge to our curiosity, yet hardly any of us can point out fifty constellations.

Not that we don't try. At one time or another we make an effort and begin to study a book about the stars but few of us ever get beyond knowing the Big Dipper.

There are, of course, plenty of books about the subject, and they do very well in most respects. But in one important point they seem to fail us: *the way they represent the constellations.*

The constellations have such intriguing names—somehow we expect the books to show us groups of stars in the shape of a Lion, a Whale, a Virgin, and so forth. But they show nothing of that sort.

Some books show, arbitrarily drawn around the stars, elaborate allegorical figures which we cannot-trace in the sky (see figure 2). Others, most of the modern ones, show the constellations as involved geometrical shapes which don't look like anything and have no relation to the names (see figure 3). Both ways are of little help if we want to find the constellations in the sky—yet this is precisely what we are after.

The result is that for most of us the constellations never come to life, and the sky remains as unfamiliar as before. Discouraged, we give up.

# TWINS, BEARS AND WHALES

This book sets out to remedy the situation. It shows the constellations in a new, graphic way, as shapes which suggest what the names imply: it shows the group of stars known as the Great Bear, in the *shape* of a bear; the Whale in the shape of a whale; the Eagle as an eagle, and so on. These shapes are easy to remember, and once you remember them you can retrace them in the sky.

In addition, the English names for the constellations are used throughout the book. In most books only the Latin and Greek names are used but words like *Taurus, Boötes,* or *Cygnus* mean little unless you are something of a linguist, while *Bull, Herdsman,* or *Swan* immediately evoke an image.[1]

The following illustrations show the new method and the ones used so far. Take for instance the TWINS (Gemini):

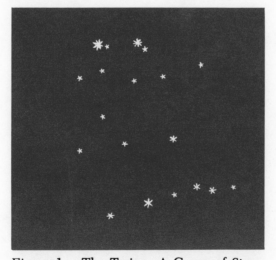

Figure 1: The Twins—A Group of Stars

These are the stars which make up the constellation as you see them in the sky, some bright, some faint, an irregular group.

[1] Many nations use native names for the constellations in popular books on the stars—the French, Germans, Italians, Russians, to mention a few with high standing in astronomy. They reserve Latin names for technical works. It's sensible to start with the familiar. If you want the Latin and Greek names, you find them all on pages 30–62, on the list on page 157, and in the index.

The books and charts which use allegorical drawings show the Twins like this:

Figure 2: The Twins—Allegorical

This may look decorative but the drawing has little to do with the stars. You cannot *see* it in the sky. It is confusing rather than helpful.

The books which use geometrical figures show the Twins somewhat like this:

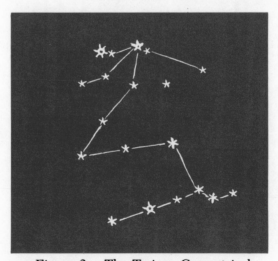

Figure 3: The Twins—Geometrical

This looks at least rational. No fancy frills. But it is a hieroglyph without a meaning. It certainly does not suggest twins. You lose track when you try to trace it in the sky, and to remember such a shape is next to impossible.

This book, which uses the new, graphic way, shows the Twins like this:

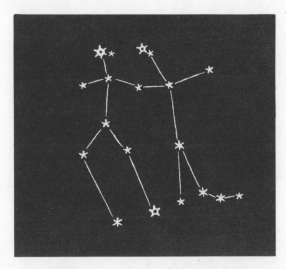

Figure 4: The Twins—Graphic

The connecting lines between the stars are drawn with a definite shape in mind, the shape which the name of the constellation suggests. The stars are exactly the same as on the other three drawings. Check them: their correct position has not been tampered with. But now the shape has a meaning: you see two matchstick men holding hands—the *Twins*. You can trace them in the sky, first with the help of the chart, and later from memory.

This graphic method has been employed throughout the book for all constellations where it was possible. Only a few—those with just two or three stars—could not be brought into a fitting shape, for obvious reasons. You can't have everything, even from the stars.

On the following two pages a few more examples are given comparing the old and the new way.

THE OLD WAY                    THE NEW WAY

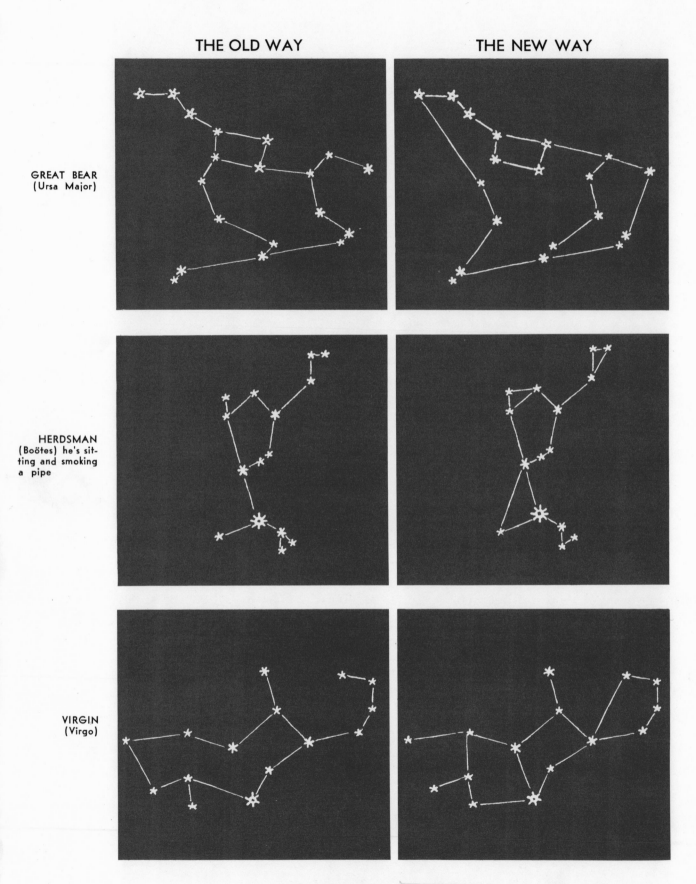

GREAT BEAR
(Ursa Major)

HERDSMAN
(Boötes) he's sit-
ting and smoking
a pipe

VIRGIN
(Virgo)

Figure 5:  Old and New
*The stars in both columns are identical; only the connecting lines are different.*

14

## THE OLD WAY　　　　THE NEW WAY

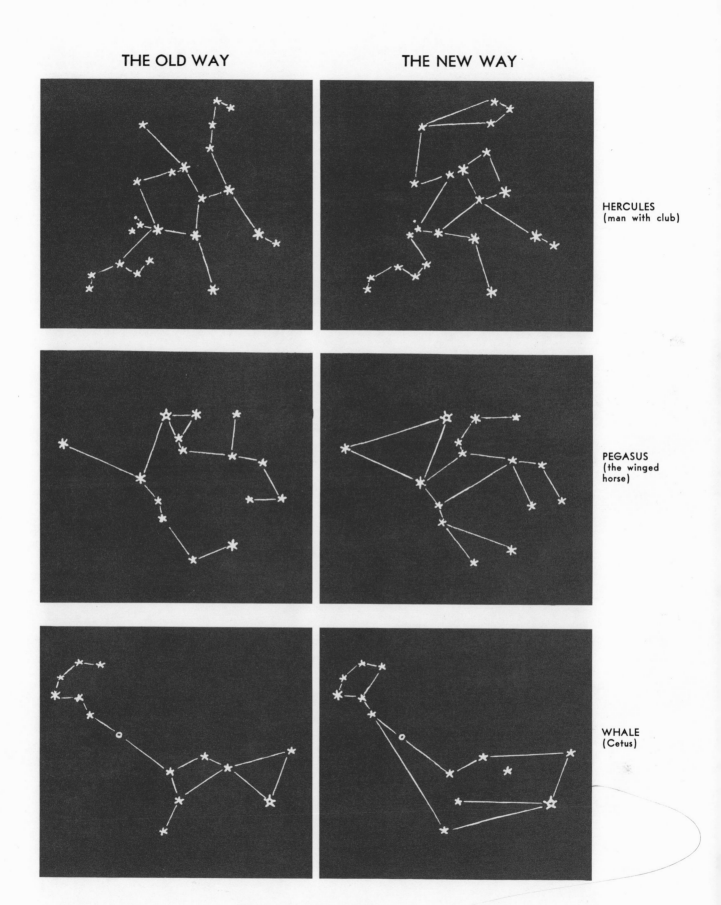

HERCULES
(man with club)

PEGASUS
(the winged horse)

WHALE
(Cetus)

Figure 6:  Old and New
*The stars in both columns are identical; only the connecting lines are different.*

15

It may even be that this new way is not so new after all.

The human eye *wants* to see shapes with a meaning. Even without intending to we see shapes of familiar things—people, animals, objects—in clouds, trees, and mountains. This is more than a pastime. It is a trend deeply rooted in the human mind, and we have good reason to believe that, long before recorded history began, man first found his way among the bewildering multitude of individual stars by *seeing figures* formed by star groups. Perhaps we are doing here precisely what he did.[1]

In Egypt and Mesopotamia where more than 5000 years ago most of our present constellations had their origin, and where no illustrated books existed for the common

reader, parents may have taught the stars to their children by drawing such figures in the sand with a stick.

But it does not matter whether they did or didn't. In past ages, men interpreted the sky after their fashion. We today are free to do likewise, and if the present interpretation makes things easier for those who want to know the stars, this book has fulfilled its purpose.

[1] A hint that our ancestors long ago *saw pictures* in the sky can be found in the fact that in all Germanic languages but English the word for constellation is literally *"star picture"*: Swedish: Stjärnbild; Norwegian: Stjernebilde; Danish: Stjernebillede; Icelandic: Stjörnumerki; German: Sternbild; Dutch: Sterrenbeeld.

**NO MATHEMATICS REQUIRED:** This is a practical book, to be used outdoors. We shall therefore limit ourselves at the start to pointing out merely *what* we can see and *where* and *when*. The *why's* can come later. If we started out with a discussion of the ecliptic, or why the sidereal day is about four minutes shorter than the solar day, your reaction might well be: Do I have to go through all this? All I want is to see the constellations! And you would be right. You can become so familiar with the stars that you can say after one glance at the sky: look, there's Arcturus! without going into mathematics or even without knowing that the earth is a globe and revolves around the sun.

No need for <u>this</u> —                    if all you want is <u>this</u> !

A plain Chaldean shepherd, more than three thousand years ago, probably knew the sky better than most of our college graduates today, yet to him the earth was a flat disc and he probably believed that the stars were little lamps carried by special deities across the solid ceiling of the sky vault every night, in strictly prescribed and never-changing formations.

*Why, stranger, you mean to say you don't know the LION?*

Only after we have done some stargazing or while we are at it do the questions of the *why* arise. Then will be the time to peruse the last part of this book—from page 107 onward—where some of those questions are briefly treated. However, if you want to go over those pages now, you are welcome to it. But don't be discouraged if all does not become clear at one reading.

And now let us start with practical steps.

**GO OUT AND LOOK:** If you want to know the stars you have to go out as often as you can and look at the sky. Pick a spot where street lights, houses, or trees don't obstruct your view too much. If you live in the city, the roof of an apartment building makes a good observatory. Clear moonless nights are ideal for stargazing, of course, because the moon has a jealous way of blotting out all faint stars. But such nights are rare, so don't wait for them. Even with some moonlight or a few clouds you can see a good number of stars. Try to make out some constellations even if they are only partly visible. Slight obstacles like these make the game only more entertaining, and it all helps to build up your acquaintance with the heavens.

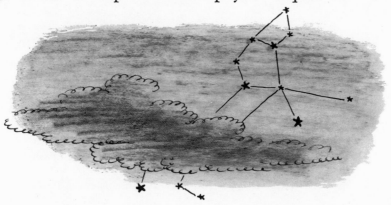

**NO EQUIPMENT NEEDED:** You need no equipment. All you have to take along is this book and a *flashlight* so you can see the charts in the dark. It's a good idea to paint the glass of the flashlight *red* with nail polish (works beautifully) because red light will not blind your eyes for the stars as white light would.

Leave your compass at home. You can find *north* easily without a compass if you know the *Big Dipper*. If you don't, almost anybody can show it to you.

You won't need field glasses either. They are fine if you want to study individual objects—the moon, planets, a nebula—but they are not much help in spotting a whole constellation because they narrow your field of vision too much. Besides, the stars which make up the constellation figures in this book can all be seen with the naked eye if the night is clear and dark.

Another thing to leave at home is the notion that stargazing is difficult. It requires less mental effort than a medium-tough crossword puzzle and is at least as much fun.

**HOW MANY STARS?** People not familiar with the skies are apt to overestimate greatly the number of stars one can see, without glasses, on a clear night. Most will guess that one can see scores of thousands but that's far off the mark. With the naked eye one sees *only about two thousand* at a time, under very best conditions. So if poets talk of millions of stars, they are either using a telescope or they exaggerate. That's their privilege and must be taken with a grain of salt.

Of course one does not have to know two thousand stars individually. They make up the constellations; that's all there is to it as far as the casual stargazer is concerned. But there are about thirty stars which are particularly bright or interesting. It is good to know those by name and to know where to find them: Sirius, Capella, Vega, for example, and also the *Pole Star* which we shall meet in a moment.

The number of constellations is not overwhelming either. There are only eighty-eight in the entire sky. About sixty can be seen in our latitudes[1] but we never see them all at once: only about two dozen are visible at any given moment. If you know *thirty constellations,* the more important ones, you have a good working knowledge of the sky. Make the acquaintance of two or three each time you go out and you will soon be familiar with all thirty.

The remaining constellations are mostly small and have no bright stars in them. They fill the chinks between the more important ones, and you will probably pick them up as you go along.

**FINDING NORTH AND THE POLE STAR:** To spot the constellations you have to take your bearings first. You find *north* without a compass with the help of the *Big Dipper.* Here is how: first you spot the Dipper; then you draw a line, in your imagination, between the two stars at the end of the bowl farthest from the handle,

[1] The only place where you can see all constellations is the equator, but even there you cannot see them all at once.

and prolong this line about 5 times, the way the sketch shows; this line will hit a fairly bright star: POLARIS, the Pole Star. You can't miss it: there are no bright stars near it. Those two stars in the Dipper's bowl are very logically called the POINTERS because they always point to the Pole Star.

The Pointers always point to Pole Star, no matter how Dipper stands

Figure 7:   Dipper and Pole Star

Polaris is a very important star because of its unique location. It is almost exactly at the pole of the sky: the point around which the whole sky appears to be moving (we shall take up that motion in a moment), and the Pole Star therefore remains, practically, always at the same place in the sky: almost *exactly north* (hence it is also called North Star) and, at a latitude of about 40° north,[1] almost halfway up in the sky; half the way, that is, from the horizon to the point directly overhead, the *zenith*. If you face the Pole Star you are facing *north*, so to your right is *east*, to your left *west*, and right behind your back you have *south*, without the help of a compass.

[1] This is, roughly, the latitude of New York, Philadelphia, Indianapolis, Denver, and Salt Lake City. The farther north you are, the higher up the Pole Star will be, and the farther south, the lower. More about that later.

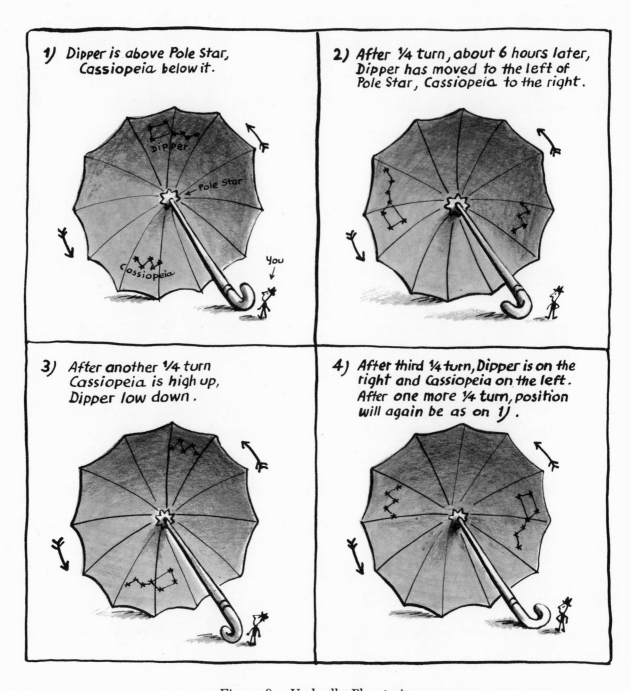

Figure 8:   Umbrella Planetarium

**UMBRELLA PLANETARIUM:** The Pole Star is the only star which keeps its place in the sky.   All the other stars and constellations wander around the pole *once daily*, counterclockwise, as though they were fixed to the inside of a vast hollow globe.

In other words, we see the whole sky slowly *rotate around the Pole Star.* (One turn takes 23 hours 56 minutes, to be more exact; these four minutes less than a day are important, as we shall see on pages 122–123, but we need not worry about them here.)

To visualize this rotation imagine a giant umbrella, with the Pole Star as its center and yourself at the handle. On the umbrella are the Big Dipper and Cassiopeia. You see them go around the Pole Star as the umbrella slowly turns.

We know of course that the sky does not really turn but that it is the earth which does the turning. The effect, however, is the same.

While the sky as a whole rotates, the stars do not change their position in relation to each other: the Pointers always point to the Pole Star, Cassiopeia is always opposite the Dipper, and so on. Therefore the stars, in contrast to the Planets, are called *Fixed Stars.*

Big Dipper, Cassiopeia, and four fainter constellations (Little Dipper, Cepheus, Dragon, Giraffe) are arranged around the pole and not very far from it. They are called CIRCUMPOLAR CONSTELLATIONS. They can be high or low in the sky as they travel around the Pole Star but they are always above the horizon. They never rise or set and can be seen at any time of the year.[1]

The constellations farther from the pole—the great majority—also travel around the pole once a day but part of the time they go below the horizon. They rise in the eastern part of the sky, travel across the sky, and set in the western part. They are out of sight for longer or shorter periods of the year. There is no use in looking for the Lion in November, for instance, or for Orion in May. (Let us just note the fact, for the moment. We shall see the "how and why" later.)

Some constellations cannot be seen at all in our latitudes because they make their whole daily turn below the horizon: the famous *Southern Cross,* for instance. To see the Cross and other far southern constellations you have to travel far south, the

[1] At a latitude of about 40° north. In the southernmost states, such as Florida, Hawaii, or in Puerto Rico and the Virgin Isles, they dip partly beneath the horizon when they are low in the sky.

farther the better. If you do, take this book along. It is designed mainly for our northern latitudes, from 30 to 50 degrees, but it also has charts to show the skies as far north as Alaska and as far south as Australia and Argentina.

There you can see the Southern Cross any night of the year, but you will look in vain for the familiar shape of the Big Dipper. No reason, though, to envy the people in Sydney or Buenos Aires. Those who have seen both, Dipper and Cross, agree that the Dipper is the finer one of the two.

The Dipper? never seen it...

# PART 2

# MEET  THE  CONSTELLATIONS

# PART TWO

# MEET THE CONSTELLATIONS

ON THE FOLLOWING seventeen charts you find the constellations, a few at a time. Study their shapes at leisure: once its shape is familiar you can spot a constellation in the sky even if you can't see it whole, just as you can recognize a friend's face even if he has got a hat on and his collar up on a cold day.

The blue field in the center of each chart merely serves to emphasize the constellations under discussion. Around that field the neighboring groups are shown to give you the context. The small numbers in circles indicate the charts where you find them discussed; you don't have to go back to the index if you want to look them up.

The stars on the charts are represented by the following symbols:

which indicate the degree of brightness, or *Magnitude*, of each star (zero, 1st, 2nd, 3rd, etc., magnitude). The lower the figure of magnitude the brighter the star. The difference in brightness between stars is great and much more pronounced in the sky than on a chart. This strikes you again and again and is something to keep in mind when you trace the constellations outdoors with the chart in hand.[1]  The fainter stars are often blotted out completely by even a slight haze, and in big cities you can see them only on exceptionally clear, moonless nights when they are high up in the sky.

Stars of zero and first magnitude (mag. for short) are usually grouped together as 1st-mag. stars.  There are 20 of these in the entire sky, and you will soon know them by name.  They are the brightest ones; you cannot fail to see them as soon as you go out at night, even before your eye has become adjusted to darkness.

Not quite as bright are the 2nd-mag. stars, about 50 in all; some of those, too, we shall come to know by name, and one we have already met: Polaris, the North Star.

The 3rd-mag. stars, about 150, are still fairly bright.  All 1st-, 2nd-, and 3rd-mag. stars are on our charts, and also more than 600 4th-mag. stars, faint by comparison but plainly visible on clear nights.  Stars of 5th mag. are about the faintest you see under good conditions; there are roughly 1500 of them (the fainter the stars the more there are of them), but less than a hundred appear on these charts—those that are not isolated but, together with brighter stars, help to form a distinct shape and thus become more easily visible, as in the Dolphin, the Cup, the Fishes, among others. No 6th-mag. stars are shown here.  Only the eagle-eyed can see them without glasses, under perfect conditions.  For anything fainter, binoculars or a telescope are needed.

Stars not only differ in brightness, they also have *different colors*.  At first glance they may all appear silverish white but a closer look reveals that quite a few are colored: bluish, reddish, yellowish, even greenish.  It is only a faint tinge but the more you study them the more you become aware of it.  A good example are bluish *Vega* and orange-colored *Arcturus*.  When you see them both in the sky at the same time you notice the contrast distinctly.

[1] The terms *mag. 0, 1, 2, 3*, etc., are only approximations.  Few stars oblige by being *exactly* mag. 0 or 1 or 2, etc.  Thus two stars of, say, 2nd mag. need not be equally bright: e.g., the star Castor, in the Twins, is of mag. 1.58, while Polaris is mag. 2.12, yet both are classed as 2nd mag.  A star of mag. 0.0 is about 2½ times as bright as one of mag. 1.0; one of mag. 1.0 is 2½ times as bright as one mag. 2.0, and so on, which means that a star of mag. 0.0 is 100 times as bright as one of mag. 5.0.  Magnitudes brighter than mag. 0 are marked by a minus sign. Only two stars are that bright: Sirius (mag. −1.58) and Canopus (mag. −0.86).

A list at the end of the book (page 160) gives you magnitude and color of the 20 brightest stars.

To the astronomer, a star's color is a clue to its physical condition and temperature. For us here, it's one more way to identify a star. Besides, it looks charming.

A mark on each chart indicates the points of the compass: north, east, south, and west. You may be puzzled to find that with north up, east is to the left and west to the right, the opposite of terrestrial maps. The reason is that terrestrial maps show the ground you are standing on while sky maps show the region overhead. Hold a sky chart over your head, and the directions will fall in place: east on east, west on west, etc.

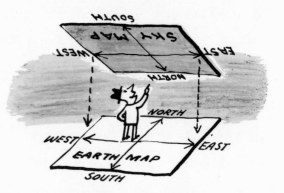

The notes on the pages opposite the charts are non-technical, and there is nothing in them that has to be memorized. If a term or a name is not familiar you will find its meaning or pronunciation in the index at the end of the book, which doubles as a glossary.

The Constellation Charts show you *what* to look for. The *where* and *when* is shown on the Calendar Charts.

# THE CONSTELLATION CHARTS

## BIG DIPPER, LITTLE DIPPER, DRAGON

**BIG DIPPER**: Best-known group of stars. We can't call it best-known constellation because it is not a constellation[1] by itself but only part of the large constellation Great Bear (see chart 3). Next to Orion it is the most impressive figure in our skies. It helps find the Pole Star and north by way of the POINTERS, the two stars at the tip of the bowl.

Close to the middle star of the handle, MIZAR, sits a tiny star, ALCOR, faint but famous. Before the age of eyeglasses and oculists' charts, Alcor used to serve as an eye test. If you could see it your vision was considered normal. Mizar and Alcor are also called "Horse and Rider."

**LITTLE DIPPER** (LITTLE BEAR—URSA MINOR): Resembles a Dipper more than a Bear, so why not stick to that name. The Little Dipper is much less conspicuous than the Big Dipper but it contains the most important star of our skies, POLARIS, the *Pole Star*, which always remains on the same spot (nearly) while all other stars circle around it. Polaris is not one of the brightest stars—only of 2nd mag. —nor was it always the star closest to the pole. On account of the "wobble" of the earth's axis (see page 128) the celestial pole slowly shifts as the centuries go by, and different stars become pole stars at different times.

Most of the Little Dipper's stars are faint. Only the two at the end of the bowl are fairly bright. They are called *Guardians of the Pole* as they march around the pole like sentries. The brighter one of the Guardians, KOCHAB, was the Pole Star at the time of Plato, about 400 B.C.

**DRAGON** (DRACO): Large constellation but not very bright. A string of stars winding around the Little Dipper makes up its long *tail,* two pairs of stars mark the legs. Its most conspicuous part is the *head,* an irregular quadrangle not quite half the size of the Big Dipper's bowl, with two fairly bright stars which look a little like the Guardians; don't confuse them.

The faint star in the Dragon's tail halfway between Mizar (the Horse and Rider) and the Guardians is THUBAN. Thuban is one of the Elder Statesmen: it was the Pole Star when the Pyramids were being built, some four or five thousand years ago. It will be the Pole Star again some twenty thousand years hence.

BIG and LITTLE DIPPER can be seen all year around. The DRAGON can best be seen from late May to early November (Calendar Charts 6, 7, 8, 9, 10).

[1] You might ask: why is the Big Dipper not a constellation? The answer is that only the 88 groups of stars that are officially recognized and listed as constellations can rightfully go by that name. The group known as the Big Dipper, famous as it is, has no official status. Such a group is called an *asterism*.

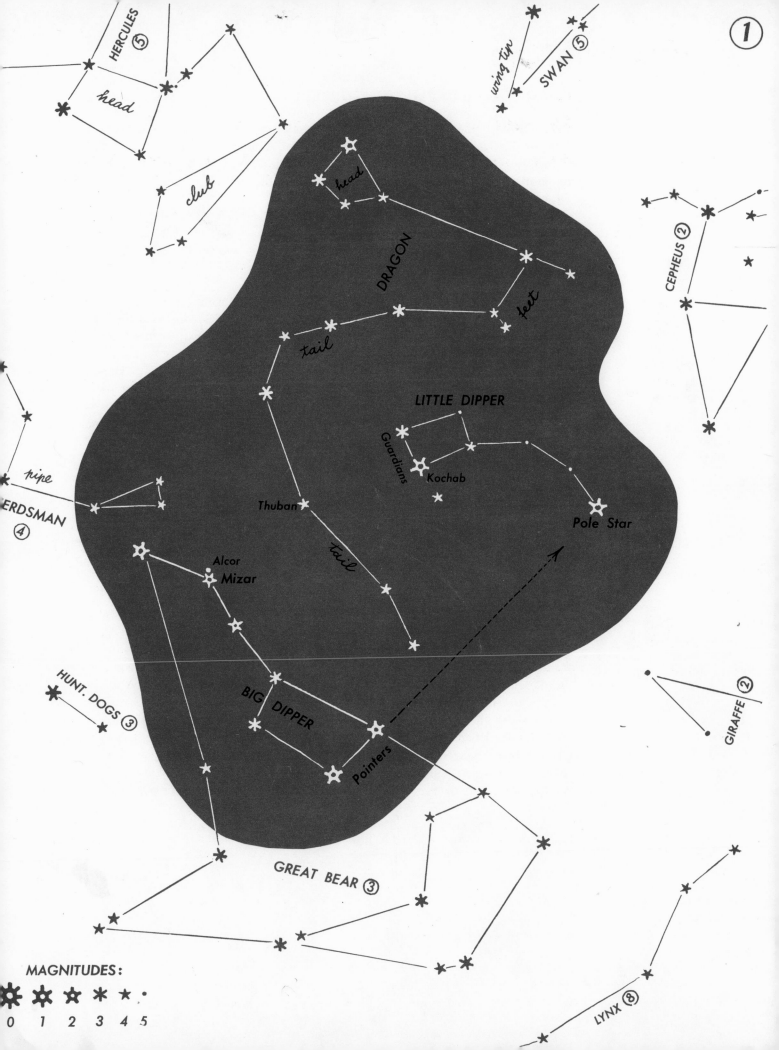

HERCULES ⑤

head

club

SWAN ⑤

wing tip

CEPHEUS ②

DRAGON

head

tail

feet

LITTLE DIPPER

Guardians

Kochab

Pole Star

Thuban

Tail

pipe

ERDSMAN ④

Alcor
Mizar

Tail

GIRAFFE ②

HUNT. DOGS ③

BIG DIPPER

Pointers

LYNX ⑧

GREAT BEAR ③

MAGNITUDES:

0  1  2  3  4  5

## CASSIOPEIA, CEPHEUS, GIRAFFE

**CASSIOPEIA:** Important constellation, not very large but bright, in the Milky Way. Next to Big Dipper and Orion, it is the constellation best known because its shape is easy to remember: a neat W formed by 5 bright stars, or an M, depending upon its position. To find Cassiopeia draw a line from the star where the handle joins the Dipper's bowl to the Pole Star and beyond.

According to myth Cassiopeia was an Ethiopian queen (see note below). The constellation is thought to represent either the queen herself or her chair, a flattering alternative. Opinions are divided on the issue, so we shall stick to the well-known "W."

**CEPHEUS:** Named after King Cepheus of Ethiopia,[1] Cassiopeia's husband. He is rather dim—his wife is much brighter—but when the constellation is not too low you can make out the large triangular cap or crown, the king's squarish face beneath it, and a sort of a pigtail at the back of the king's head.

To find Cepheus, continue the line from the Pointers beyond the Pole Star: it hits the king's cap (see chart). Cepheus is in the Milky Way, partly, and his three brighter stars are all candidates for the pole starship, 2000, 4000, and 6000 years from now (see figure 24, page 129), and Cepheus will then be a very important person.

**GIRAFFE** (CAMELOPARDALIS): Faint constellation, hard to spot and not worth bothering with unless you are a perfectionist. It is a *modern* constellation, a term explained on page 147.

**BEST TIMES** for CASSIOPEIA and CEPHEUS: August through January.
GIRAFFE: November through March.
Being circumpolar constellations they are on all twelve Calendar Charts.

NOTE: There is a myth about Cassiopeia and some adjoining constellations which helps to remember them as being together in the same section of the sky: Cassiopeia and Cepheus had a daughter, *Andromeda* (see chart 6). Cassiopeia's boasting about Andromeda's beauty so angered the sea nymphs that they prevailed upon the sea god Poseidon to dispatch a sea monster, the *Whale* (chart 15), to ravage Ethiopia's coast. To appease the Whale, Cepheus had Andromeda chained to a rock to be devoured by the monster. Fortunately the hero, *Perseus* (chart 7), happened to pass by. He killed the Whale, liberated and married Andromeda, and the two made off on Perseus' winged horse, *Pegasus* (chart 6).

When Cassiopeia is high up in the sky, in late fall and early winter, Cepheus, Andromeda, Perseus, Pegasus, and the Whale can also be seen well.

[1] Some have identified this mythological king (*Kepheus* in Greek spelling) with the Egyptian Pharaoh *Cheops,* or *Khufu,* ca. 2700 B.C., of pyramid fame. Such matters of mythology are hard to prove or disprove, but it's a plausible thought.

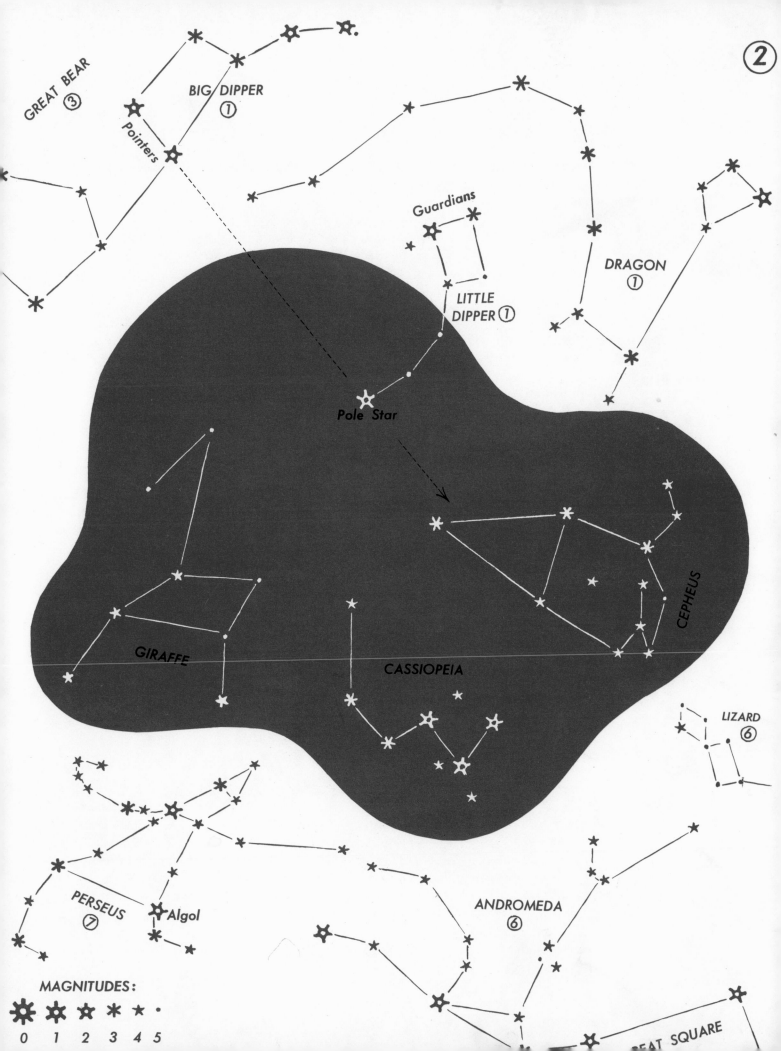

GREAT BEAR ③

BIG DIPPER ①

Pointers

Guardians

LITTLE DIPPER ①

DRAGON ①

Pole Star

GIRAFFE

CASSIOPEIA

CEPHEUS

LIZARD ⑥

PERSEUS ⑦

Algol

ANDROMEDA ⑥

GREAT SQUARE

MAGNITUDES:

0  1  2  3  4  5

②

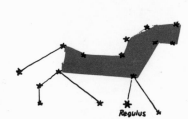

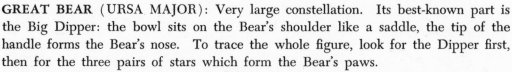

## GREAT BEAR, LION, HUNTING DOGS, LITTLE LION

**GREAT BEAR** (URSA MAJOR): Very large constellation. Its best-known part is the Big Dipper: the bowl sits on the Bear's shoulder like a saddle, the tip of the handle forms the Bear's nose. To trace the whole figure, look for the Dipper first, then for the three pairs of stars which form the Bear's paws.

The Greek word for bear is *arktos*, hence the name *Arctic*, literally *bearish*, for the far northern parts of the earth where the Great Bear appears even more dominant than in our latitudes.

**LION** (LEO): Large constellation with three bright stars. The brightest one, REGULUS, is easy to find when the Big Dipper is high up: use the two stars of the Dipper's bowl next to the handle and draw a straight line toward the Bear's paws and beyond; it will first hit the star in the Lion's shoulder and then Regulus. Bluish-white Regulus is the faintest of our 1st-mag. stars but even so it shines about twice as bright as Polaris. It is about 80 light-years away and over 100 times as luminous as the sun.

The Lion's bright tail-light is the star DENEBOLA, interesting because it forms, with Arcturus (chart 4), Cor Caroli, and Spica (chart 11), the *Virgin's Diamond* (see Calendar Chart 3).

The Lion is in the *Zodiac*, a belt formed by 12 constellations girdling the sky (see page 130 for fuller explanation). Sun, moon, and planets always travel within this belt, so at one time or another you may expect to see a planet in the Lion, or even more than one.

Along the middle of the zodiac runs the *ecliptic,* the apparent path of the sun among the stars through the year (see page 119)—an imaginary line, of course—and Regulus is almost exactly on it. The moon, which crosses the ecliptic at regular intervals, may occasionally pass in front of Regulus and hide it: an interesting sight, called *occultation* and more fully described on page 139.

The Lion's front part is known as the SICKLE, and it looks like one.

**HUNTING DOGS** (CANES VENATICI): Small modern constellation with only two naked-eye stars. The brighter one, COR CAROLI (Charles' Heart after Charles II of England), belongs to the four stars which form the Virgin's Diamond (see above).

**LITTLE LION** (LEO MINOR): Small modern constellation, very faint, looks like a mouse rather than a lion's cub.

**BEST TIME:** February through June; Calendar Charts 2 to 6.

NOTE: You become familiar with the sky more easily if you remember some constellations *in groups.* The constellations shown here all represent carnivores: Great Bear, Big and Little Lion, Hunting Dogs; and also Lynx, Dragon, and Little Bear adjoining them. This region of the sky could be called *Carnivores' Corner.* It is best seen from early spring to early summer. Crutch for memory: bears hibernate; the other carnivores in the sky follow their example, therefore they are harder to find during fall and early winter.

*sorry - no shape only two stars*

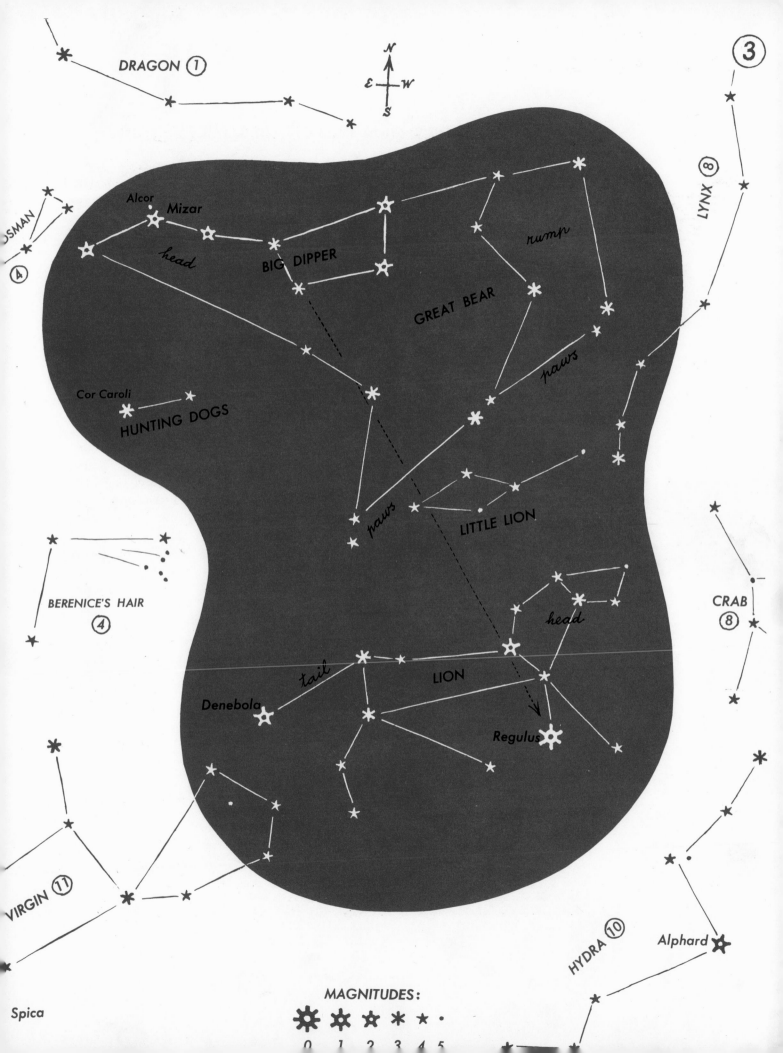

## HERDSMAN, NORTHERN CROWN, BERENICE'S HAIR

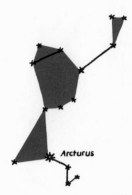

**HERDSMAN** (BOÖTES): Among the oldest recorded constellations. Looks like a man sitting and smoking a pipe, a sensible thing for a herdsman to do. Its main star, orange-colored ARCTURUS, is the sixth brightest of all the stars. You find Arcturus easily if you follow the sweep of the Big Dipper's handle, away from the bowl.

Arcturus is remarkable not so much because it opened the Chicago World's Fair in 1934 by shining on a photoelectric cell, but because it changes its place in the sky more rapidly than any other of the bright stars. It moves toward the Virgin by about one degree (which is about twice the apparent width of a full moon) in 1600 years, so at the time of the Battle of Hastings it was about one full moon's width farther northeast in the sky than it is now. Besides it is a giant star, about 25 times the diameter of the sun, and 100 times as luminous. It is a relatively close neighbor of ours, only 40 light-years away.[1] In late spring and early summer, Arcturus is the first star you see after sunset, high up in the sky.

To trace the rest of the constellation, try to find the triangular body first, then the large head, then the pipe close to the Bear's nose, then the tiny feet. Pipe and feet are rather faint; it takes a clear night to see them.

**NORTHERN CROWN** (CORONA BOREALIS): Small but graceful. Looks rather like a tiara, with 2nd-mag. GEMMA, the Crown Jewel, in the middle of the bow. The Dipper's handle—or the Bear's nose if you prefer—points toward Gemma, beyond the Herdsman's head.

**BERENICE'S HAIR** (COMA BERENICES): Small and very faint. Contains a group of dim stars, visible only on clear, moonless nights when the constellation is high up. Shown here as a few strands of hair fluttering from a stick between the star Cor Caroli and the Virgin's outstretched arm.

This constellation owes its name to a theft: Berenice was an Egyptian queen (3rd century B.C.) who sacrificed her hair to thank Venus for a victory her husband had won in a war. The hair was stolen from the temple but the priests in charge convinced the disconsolate queen that Zeus himself had taken the locks and put them in the sky as a constellation.

Of all our constellations, Berenice's Hair is the one farthest from the *Milky Way*. With the queen's hair overhead you don't see the Milky Way: it then runs along the horizon, blotted out by the atmosphere near the ground. Thus no hair can ever get into the milk, celestially speaking.

**BEST TIME**: April through August. Calendar Charts 3 to 8.

---

[1] A LIGHT–YEAR—a measure of space, not of time—is the distance light travels in a year: about six million million miles. Forty light-years is not much, in stellar terms. More about light-years, luminosity, motions, and distances of stars on pages 141–142.

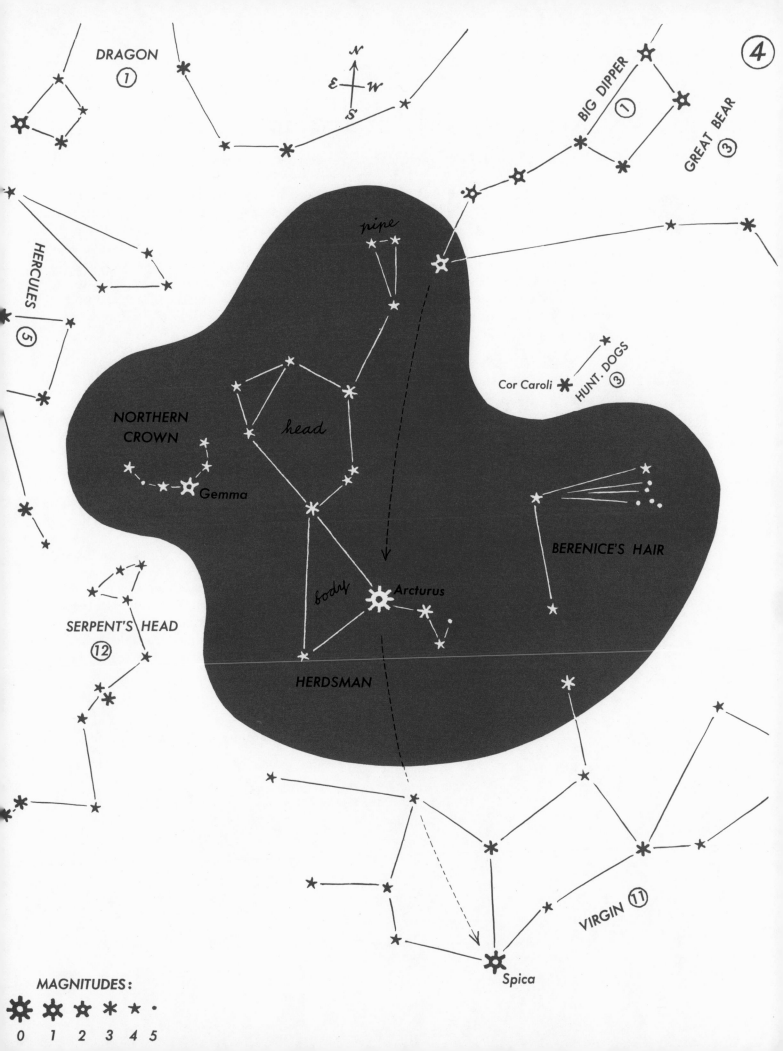

## LYRE, SWAN, HERCULES, LITTLE FOX

**LYRE (LYRA):** Small constellation, looking more like a two-stringed zither than a traditional lyre. The Lyre is important because VEGA, fourth brightest of all the stars, is in it, brilliant and bluish white. Vega is below the horizon only about 7 hours daily and you can see it any night of the year, though not always at convenient hours.[1] Like Arcturus, Vega is a close neighbor of ours; only 23 light-years away, it is some 50 times as luminous as the sun, and we are moving toward it at 12 miles a second. We should bump into Vega within 500,000 years (a negligible span, astronomically speaking) if Vega did not move too. In 12,000 years Vega will be the Pole Star, and stargazing will then be easy, with a pivotal star as brilliant as that. In addition, Vega was the first star to have its photograph taken, in 1850, over a century ago. The Dragon's head, not far away, points toward Vega.

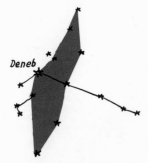

**SWAN (CYGNUS):** Large magnificent constellation. Part of it is known as the NORTHERN CROSS: this part is drawn in slightly heavier lines on the chart. The Swan's wings are spread wide, his neck is stretched out, and his feet, formed by fainter stars, are trailing behind as he flies along the Milky Way.

The brightest star in the Swan is DENEB, white, in the tail. Deneb is below the horizon only about 5 hours daily and, like Vega, can be seen at some time any night of the year. It is almost 500 light-years away, and its candle power must be enormous to make it shine as bright as it does, at this distance: it is supposed to be 10,000 times as luminous as the sun.

A line through the two stars of the Dipper's bowl near the handle and far across the sky leads to Deneb (see sketch below).

**HERCULES:** Large but rather dim and therefore a bit hard to trace. It looks like a man swinging a club, Hercules' favorite weapon. Best way to spot him is by tracing his head first: a keystone-shaped quadrangle, halfway between Vega and Gemma (in the Crown). On very clear nights you may see, on the spot marked on the chart by a tiny cross, a faint, hazy star. This is no single star, though, but a cluster of many thousands of stars, almost 35,000 light-years away: the Great Cluster of Hercules.

**LITTLE FOX (VULPECULA):** Small modern constellation; don't bother.

**BEST TIMES** for LYRE: May through November.
                SWAN: June through November.
                HERCULES: May through October.
                Calendar Charts 5 to 12.

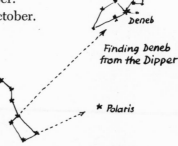

Finding Deneb from the Dipper

★ Polaris

[1] At latitude 40°, that is. In southern Florida (about 25°) Vega will be below the horizon for over 9 hours, but in Alaska it never sets, nor does Deneb.

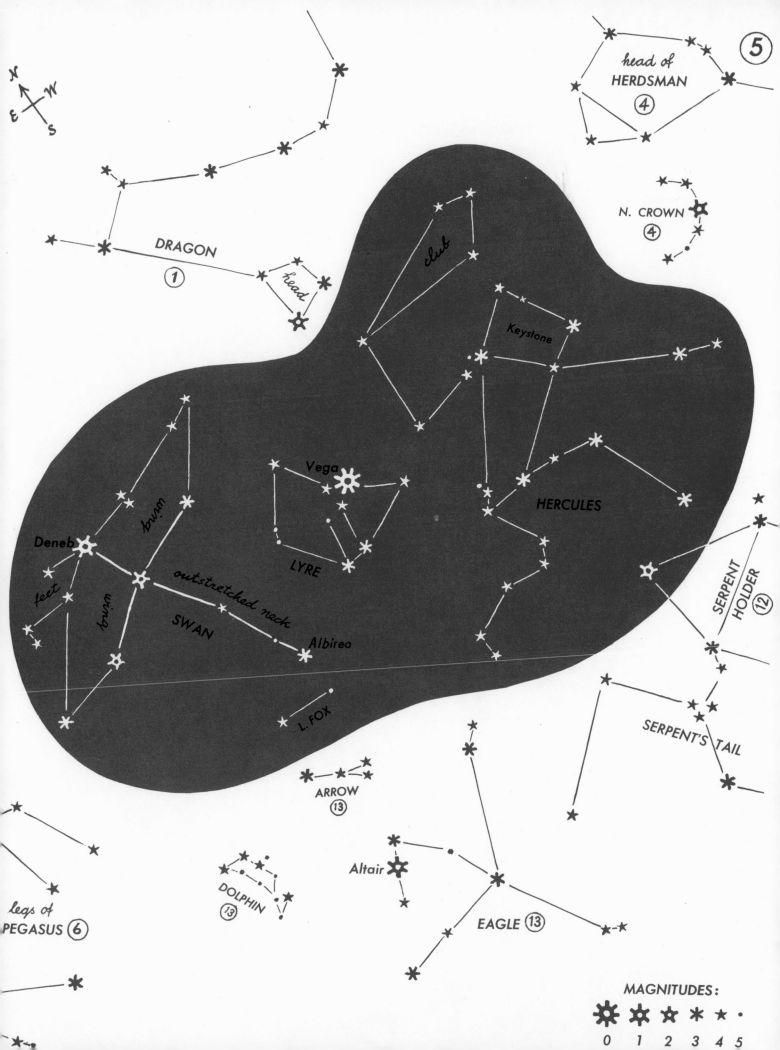

**5**

head of
HERDSMAN
④

DRAGON
①

head

club

Keystone

N. CROWN
④

HERCULES

Vega

LYRE

Deneb

brum

outstretched neck

feet

brum

SWAN

Albireo

SERPENT
HOLDER
⑫

SERPENT'S TAIL

L. FOX

legs of
PEGASUS ⑥

ARROW
⑬

DOLPHIN
⑬

Altair

EAGLE ⑬

MAGNITUDES:

0   1   2   3   4   5

# GREAT SQUARE, ANDROMEDA, PEGASUS, TRIANGLE, LIZARD

**GREAT SQUARE OF PEGASUS:** One of the landmarks of the sky. It is not a constellation in itself [1] but belongs partly to ANDROMEDA, partly to PEGASUS, and helps find both. It is formed by four bright stars. Two of these stars are on a straight line drawn from the Pole Star to the last star in Cassiopeia's W (see chart) and beyond. [2] If you have the right Calendar Chart before you, outdoors, you find the Square easily, and once you know it you won't forget it, it's such a striking figure.

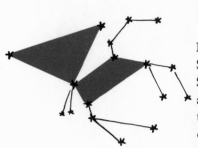

**ANDROMEDA—THE CHAINED LADY:** On this chart, the lady is standing on her head, which is one of the four stars of the Square. Spot first the three bright stars forming one side of the body and one leg, and then the rest. The other leg is formed by dimmer stars. At its bent knee you see a small hazy spot, if the night is perfectly clear and moonless: this is the famous ANDROMEDA NEBULA, the most distant object the human eye can see unaided. It is a *galaxy* like our own, composed of some hundred billion suns and about 2.7 million light-years away. This is a case where glasses are a help because the spot is very faint. More about galaxies on page 143.

For the *Andromeda myth* see note on page 32. The chain which fastened the princess to the rock is dangling from her outstretched arm, and on the lower left of the chart you see the snout of the Whale, sent out to devour her.

**PEGASUS—THE WINGED HORSE:** Trace this constellation from the corner of the Square opposite Andromeda's head. The triangular wing, made up of three of the Square's four stars, is fastened to the Horse's rump. This will look unorthodox to airplane designers but the Horse manages to fly all right. The star at the forward tip of the wing is reddish. Pegasus is not as bright as Andromeda but under good conditions one can trace it well.

**TRIANGLE (TRIANGULUM):** Tiny figure just off Andromeda's brighter foot.

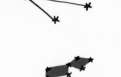

**LIZARD (LACERTA):** Small modern constellation, very faint, in Milky Way.

**BEST TIMES** for SQUARE: August to January.
                ANDROMEDA: September to January.
                PEGASUS: August to October.
                Calendar Charts 1, 2, 8 to 12.

---

[1] While the impressive Great Square is only an asterism (see note on page 30) there is also a true constellation called the SQUARE (NORMA), a faint little group in the southern sky (Constellation Chart 17). It seems a bit unfair, but that's the way things go, at times, in astronomy.

[2] This line hits the snout of the WHALE if you draw it farther south. It's an interesting line because it marks, roughly, the ZERO HOUR CIRCLE. Hour circles are to the sky globe what meridians or circles of longitude are to the terrestrial globe, and the zero hour circle is so to speak the Greenwich line of the sky. More about hour circles and related items on page 114.

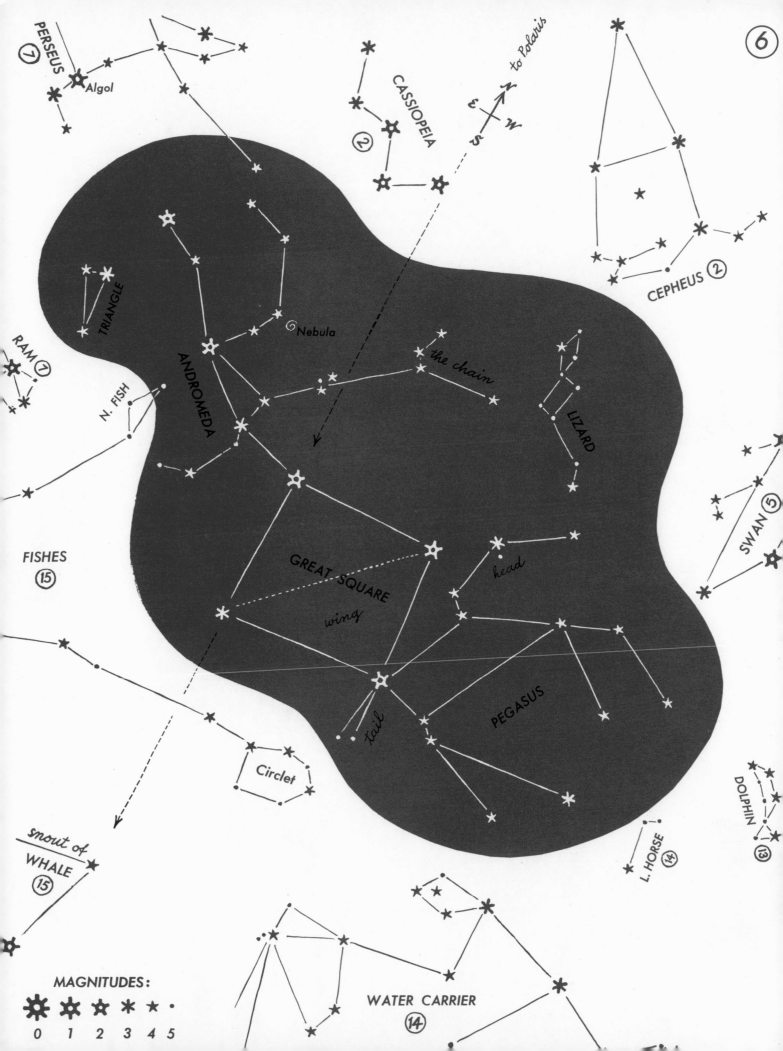

PERSEUS ⑦

Algol

CASSIOPEIA ②

to Polaris

N
E
W
S

CEPHEUS ②

TRIANGLE

RAM ①

N. FISH

ANDROMEDA

Nebula

the chain

LIZARD

SWAN ⑤

FISHES
⑮

GREAT SQUARE

wing

head

DOLPHIN ⑬

Circlet

PEGASUS

tail

L. HORSE ⑭

snout of
WHALE
⑮

WATER CARRIER
⑭

MAGNITUDES:

0  1  2  3  4  5

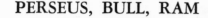

## PERSEUS, BULL, RAM

**PERSEUS:** Interesting constellation, in the Milky Way. Perseus is close to Cassiopeia, his mother-in-law-to-be (chart 2), and to Andromeda, his future bride (chart 6). He looks like a man with a pointed cap, a Persian cap if you like. With one hand he makes a beckoning gesture, with the other he seems about to grab Andromeda's foot: a rough way to liberate a lady.

There are two stars of second magnitude in Perseus. One of them, in his forward leg, is ALGOL (Arabic for Prankster), a famous variable star.[1] For about 2½ days Algol is of second magnitude, then dims down in about 5 hours to third magnitude, and in another 5 hours regains its former brilliance. You can observe the spectacle, with a little patience; look at it off and on during each night for a few nights in a row.

If you enjoy the sight of shooting stars, watch the sky around Perseus after midnight, between August 1 and August 30, for the *Perseïd Meteors.*

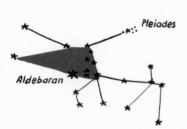

**BULL** (TAURUS): Large constellation in the zodiac, best known because of the PLEIADES. This group of faint stars looks, at first glance, like a tiny silver cloud, but watching closer you can distinguish 6 individual starlets. The Pleiades are unmistakable, and ALDEBARAN, the Bull's brightest star, is not far off, easy to spot because of its orange color. From there, trace the rest of the constellation. The hind part of the Bull is much dimmer than the large head. The Bull, supposedly, is Zeus in disguise, swimming through the Hellespont to fetch his girl friend Europa; his hind quarters are dim because they are submerged. Aldebaran is a giant star, 36 times the diameter of the sun, 100 times as luminous, and 55 light-years away.

Aldebaran and Pleiades are both near the ecliptic, so you may expect planets nearby, and both are occasionally hidden by the moon. Close to Aldebaran, in the Bull's neck, is a group of stars known as the HYADES. Both Pleiades and Hyades are clusters of stars traveling together through space. (For more about *ecliptic, planets, zodiac,* see pages 118 ff.)

**RAM** (ARIES): This constellation is rather inconspicuous and would be less famous if it were not in the zodiac. Its two brightest stars, in the Ram's head, can be spotted easily halfway between the Pleiades and the Great Square of Pegasus.

**BEST TIMES** for PERSEUS: November through March.
BULL: October through March.
RAM: October through February.
Calendar Charts 1, 2, 3, 10, 11, and 12.

[1] Algol is a double star, or BINARY (see page 141): two stars revolving around each other, and rather close together. One star is bright, the other much darker; when the dark star gets in front of the brighter one, as seen from the earth, Algol dims down.

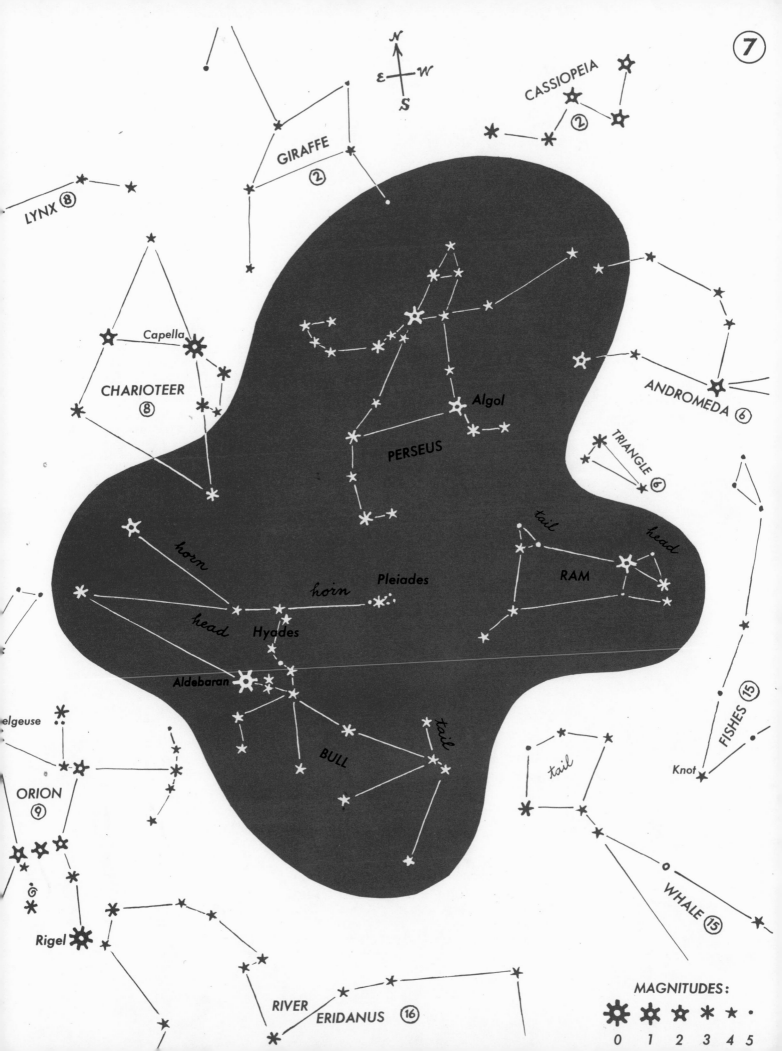

## TWINS, CHARIOTEER, LITTLE DOG, CRAB, LYNX

**THE TWINS (GEMINI):** Important group. The heads of the Twins are the bright stars CASTOR (white) and POLLUX (yellowish; brighter than Castor). To find the pair from the Dipper, draw a diagonal through the bowl and far beyond (see sketch). The stars in their arms and bodies are fainter than those in their heads and feet; you need a clear night to trace the whole figure. The Twins are in the zodiac where moon and planets travel. If the moon and a planet are near Castor and Pollux you have an impressive show. Incidentally, 2 of our 9 planets were discovered when passing through the Twins: Uranus (1781) and Pluto (1930).

**CHARIOTEER (AURIGA):** Important constellation, named after the mythical inventor of the chariot, shaped like a face under a pointed cap. Blunt nose and jutting chin give it a tough expression, as befits the driver of a war cart. The Charioteer's eye is brilliant CAPELLA, yellowish, almost as bright as Vega, 16 times as large across as the sun, 150 times as luminous, and 42 light-years away. Being relatively close to the Pole it goes below the horizon for less than 5 hours daily,[1] and can be seen, for a short while at least, any night of the year. To find Capella from the Dipper go back from the handle along the bowl's edge and straight on from there: you can't miss (see sketch). Near Capella you find three fainter stars forming the nose,[2] and then the rest.

**LITTLE DOG (CANIS MINOR):** Small but important. Its two bright stars defeat all attempts to show it as a dog or even a puppy, but it has one of the brightest stars of our skies, yellowish-white PROCYON. A sweep from Capella backward to the bright star at the rear of the cap, then onward through Castor and Pollux and beyond (see dotted line on chart), hits Procyon. Sirius (chart 9) is farther along on that same sweep. Procyon is a close neighbor of ours, 10½ light-years away, five times as luminous as the sun, and approaching us by 150 miles a minute. Its name (Greek) means "before the dog": at 40° latitude it rises about 40 minutes before Sirius, the Dog Star.

**CRAB (CANCER):** Faintest of all constellations in the zodiac. Its main attraction is the so-called BEEHIVE, a small hazy spot (marked by a cross on the chart), just visible without glasses under best conditions. Glasses reveal a cluster of many faint stars.

**LYNX:** Faint modern group near the Bear's rump. Hard to visualize as a lynx unless he's half hidden with only the back showing, sneaking up on his prey; the Little Lion, perhaps.

**BEST TIMES** for TWINS and LITTLE DOG: December through May.
        CHARIOTEER: October through April.
        CRAB and LYNX: January through May.
        Calendar Charts 1, 2, 3, 4, 5, 11, and 12.

[1] At latitude 40°, that is. In Alaska, Capella never sets, like Deneb and Vega (page 38).

[2] The Star nearest Capella, Epsilon Aurigae, is a double star. The larger of the two, itself invisible, dims the brighter one for a period of over 700 days, whence its diameter was found to be 2700 times that of the sun. It is the largest star known so far.

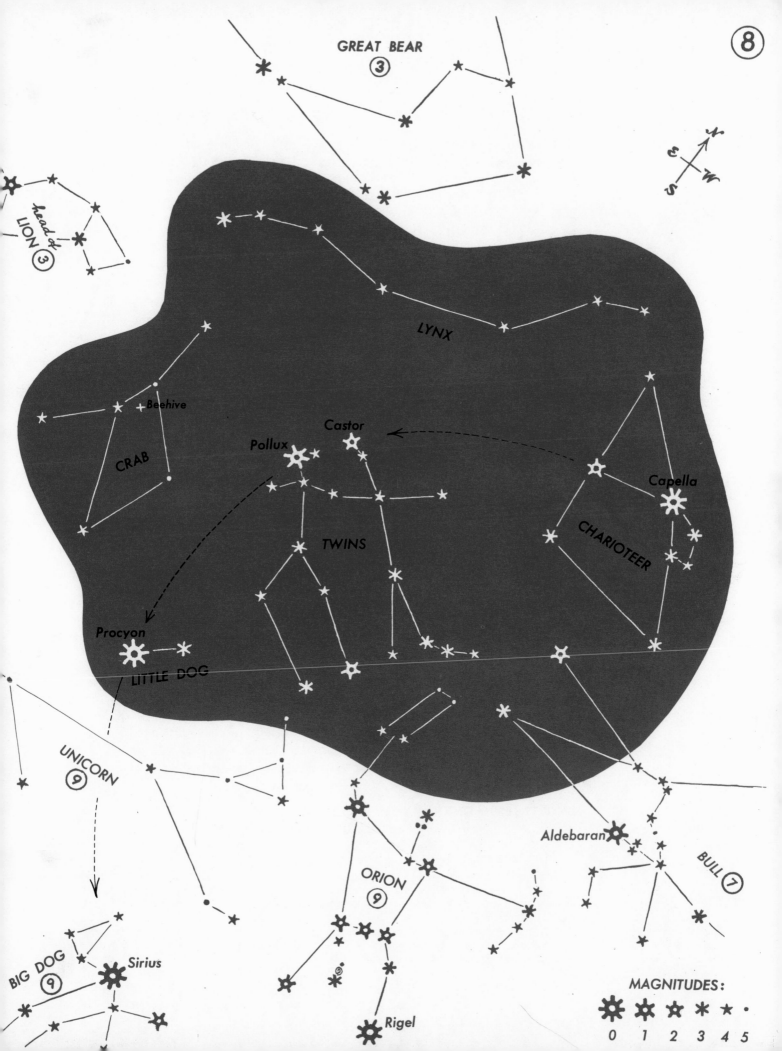

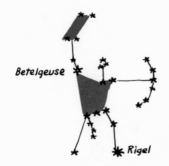

Betelgeuse

Rigel

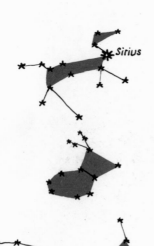

Sirius

## ORION, BIG DOG, HARE, UNICORN, ERIDANUS RIVER

**ORION:** Superb constellation. When Orion is up he dominates the southern sky, you can't miss him. His most striking part is the BELT, three bright stars in a straight row; you easily trace the rest of the constellation from there.—A hunter by profession, Orion is heavily armed, with a raised club, a shield, and a sword dangling from his belt. No other constellation has so many bright stars, five of 2nd mag. and two of 1st mag.: reddish BETELGEUSE in the left shoulder, and bluish-white RIGEL in the right foot. Rigel is a giant star, 33 times the diameter of the sun and 20,000 times as luminous, over 500 light-years away: what you see in the sky these nights is light which left the star before Columbus was born. Betelgeuse is a supergiant,[1] 400 times the sun's diameter, 3600 times as luminous, about 300 light-years away. One of the stars in Orion's sword looks slightly fuzzy; field glasses reveal a hazy spot around it: the GREAT ORION NEBULA, a luminous gas-cloud, extremely thin but so vast that 10,000 stars the size of our sun could be formed from its mass. It looks so small because it is 300 light-years away. For the *Orion myth* see page 52.

**BIG DOG** (CANIS MAJOR): Fine constellation but so far south that it takes a very clear night to see its fainter stars in our latitudes. Its brightest star, however, outshines all others in the whole sky: SIRIUS, the DOG STAR, one of our closest neighbors among the stars, is only 8½ light-years distant. Hence its brightness, though it is only 26 times as luminous as our sun. Its magnitude is negative: minus 1.6.

**HARE** (LEPUS): Modest constellation, but quite graceful. Its head is brighter than its body and easy to spot on clear nights. Orion's sword points toward it. The Hare's ears point toward the star Rigel. The shape of a sitting hare becomes clear if you twist the chart and look at the figure from the lower left.

**UNICORN** (MONOCEROS): Modern constellation, large but very dull. Don't bother.

**ERIDANUS RIVER:** Large but rather faint and shapeless. It just meanders, like a river, through one of the poorer regions of the sky. At a latitude of 40° only part of the constellation can be seen, and its only bright star, 1st-mag. ACHERNAR (chart 16), becomes visible only in the southernmost states.[2]

NOTE: The region around Orion is the most splendid of our skies. When Orion is high up, you see seven 1st-mag. stars in this relatively small section. Six of them form a vast hexagon: Capella, Pollux, Procyon, Sirius, Rigel, and Aldebaran (see Calendar Chart 1). In the center of the hexagon, more or less, you have brilliant Betelgeuse. The region to the right of Orion's feet contrasts sharply with that splendor: it is the "Wet Region," with Eridanus River, Whale, Water Carrier, and Fishes, none of them having very bright stars.

**BEST TIMES** for ORION: December through March.
BIG DOG and HARE: January through March.
Calendar Charts 1, 2, 3, 4, and 12.

---

[1] Stars with diameters from 10 to 100 times that of the sun are called giant stars; those with diameters greater than 100 times that of the sun are supergiants. Giant Rigel is so much more luminous than supergiant Betelgeuse that it appears the brighter one to us, although much farther away and of smaller size.

[2] The 4th-mag. star in Eridanus, nearest the right edge of the chart, is Epsilon ($\epsilon$) Eridani, a close neighbor, only 10⅓ light-years away. This star is similar to the sun but smaller, and astronomers hope to find out, by radio telescope, whether it has planets.

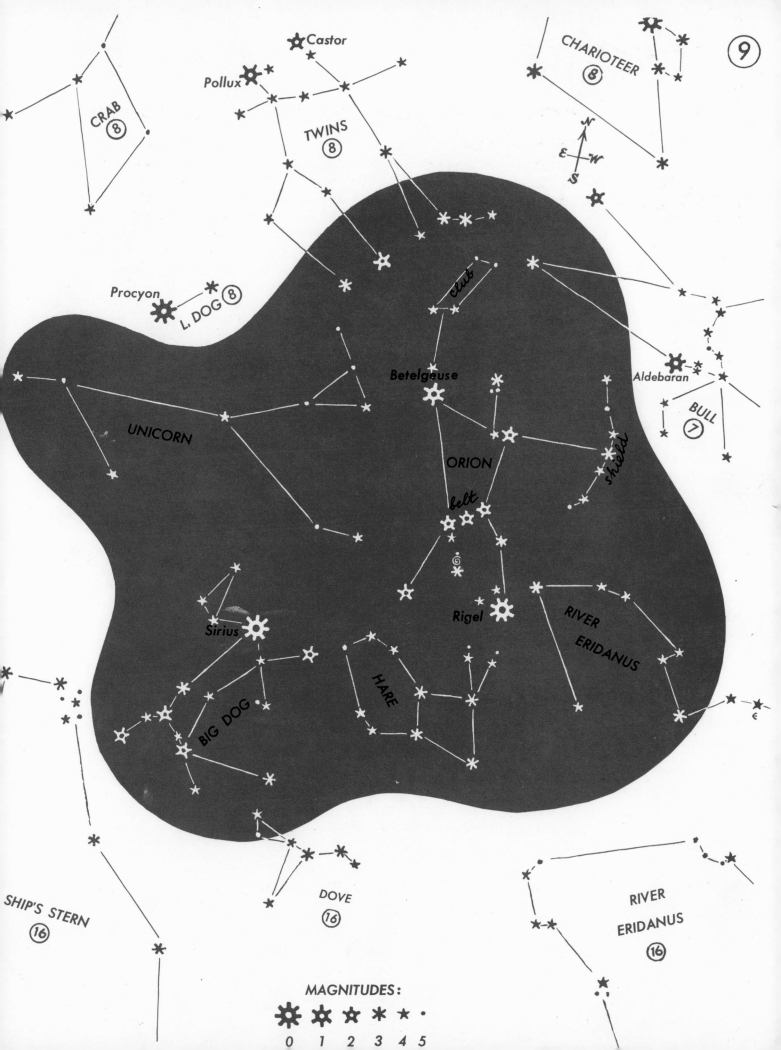

## HYDRA, CUP

**HYDRA**—The WATER SNAKE: Largest constellation of our skies and so long it does not fit into one chart: its tail is to be found on the following chart. It spans about one quarter of the sky but has little to show besides mere length. It has only one bright star—ALPHARD, of 2nd mag.—which appears brighter than it is because it has no competition near.

Hydra's head, however, is a pretty little group of stars and worth looking for: about halfway between Regulus in the Lion and Procyon in the Little Dog: a line through the stars which form the Lion's forepaws will hit Hydra's head.[1]

On the back of Hydra sits the **CUP** (CRATER), a small and rather faint constellation. It is hard to see in middle latitudes but farther south, where it rises higher, its graceful shape can be traced easily on clear dark nights.

The Snake, the Cup, and the Crow (chart 11) are connected by myth: the Crow or Raven, as it is also called, used to be the messenger of the god Apollo. Sent by the god to fetch a drink of water in the cup, the crow dallied under a fig tree till the figs were ripe enough to eat, then came home without the cup, but with the snake in his fangs as an alibi for the unaccomplished mission. Thereupon the angry god put snake, cup, and crow into the sky among the stars, and since that day all crows, formerly silvery white, are as black as night.

The solitary 4th-mag. star below Cup and Hydra belongs to the **PUMP** (ANTLIA),[2] a dull modern constellation whose other stars are too faint to be shown on this chart. Don't bother.

**BEST TIMES** for HYDRA'S HEAD: February through May.
CUP: April and May.
Calendar Charts 2 to 5.

[1] The star at the end of the Unicorn's tail, below Hydra's head, belongs technically to Hydra. Originally part of the Unicorn, it was transferred to Hydra when all constellation boundaries were revised in 1930 (see page 147). The design shown here leaves both (Hydra and Unicorn) in better shapes, but remember Hydra's claim if you are doing some serious observing.

[2] This constellation used to be called Antlia Pneumatica, the Air Pump, but astronomers have shortened it to Antlia, which means just Pump.

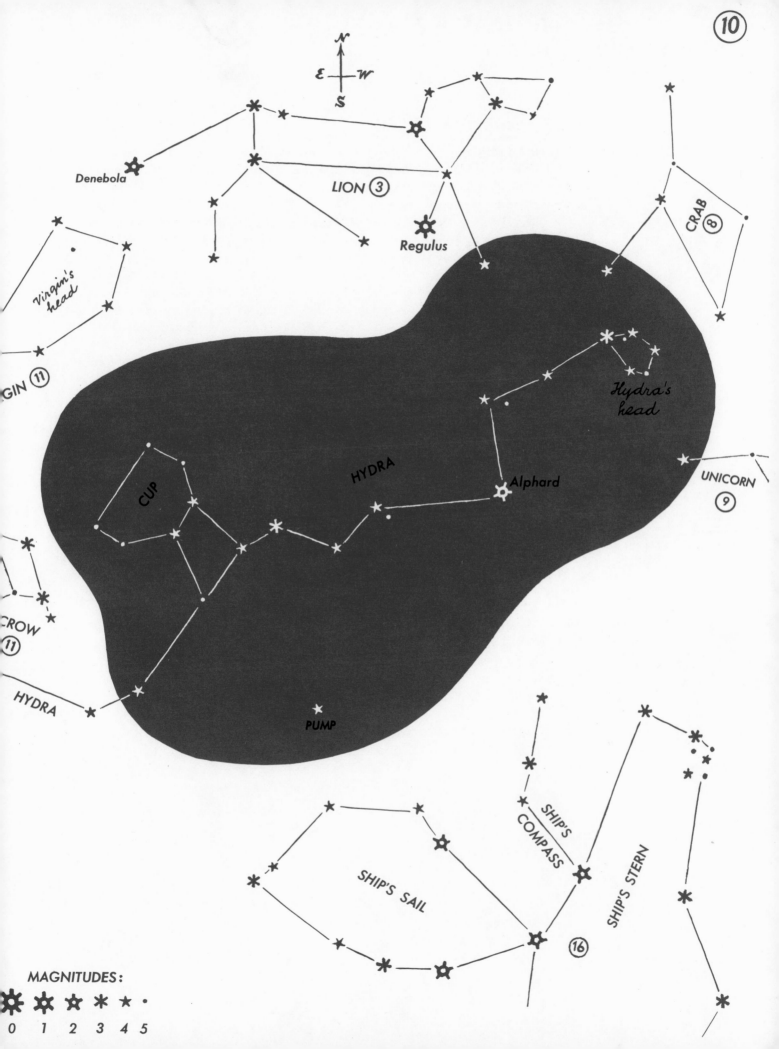

N
E W
S

Denebola

LION 3

CRAB 8

Virgin's head

VIRGIN 11

Regulus

Hydra's head

HYDRA

Alphard

UNICORN 9

CUP

CROW 11

HYDRA

PUMP

SHIP'S SAIL

SHIP'S COMPASS

SHIP'S STERN

16

MAGNITUDES:

0 1 2 3 4 5

## VIRGIN, SCALES, CROW

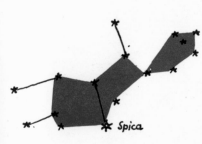

**VIRGIN** (VIRGO): Large constellation but mostly faint. She is lying on her back, stretched out along the ecliptic (see Calendar Chart 5), with her head under the Lion's tail and her arm reaching for Berenice's Hair. She seems to be looking toward the Herdsman but he turns his back on her. She carries her brightest jewel—the bluish 1st-mag. star SPICA—on an unusual spot. To find Spica, follow the sweep of the Dipper's handle to Arcturus (see chart 4) and go on with that sweep: you can't miss Spica, as there are no very bright stars near it.

However, there may be a planet nearby as the Virgin is a constellation of the zodiac. The star Spica is very close to the ecliptic; like Aldebaran, Regulus, and Antares (in the Scorpion) it is sometimes hidden by the passing moon. Spica is not a giant star, only 5 times as large across as the sun but 1000 times as luminous, and about 190 light-years away.

Spica, Arcturus, Cor Caroli (chart 3) and the Lion's tail star Denebola form the *Virgin's Diamond* (see Calendar Chart 3).

**THE SCALES** (LIBRA): Well known by name for being in the zodiac but not much to look at. It has no bright stars and the shape of a pair of scales is not easy to bring out. The star lowest to the right has a very faint greenish hue: the only green naked-eye star.

**CROW** (CORVUS): Small but quite bright, below the Virgin's head. The star at the tip of the bill, and the one where the leg joins the bird's body, are rather faint, so the complete shape of a sitting crow can only be seen under best conditions, but the four brightest stars of the constellation, forming a quadrangle, are easily found. The Crow's bill is pointed toward the Virgin's jewel, Spica, as though he were waiting for a chance to grab it.

NOTE: South of Hydra's tail lie the WOLF, CENTAUR, and the famous SOUTHERN CROSS (chart 17), too far south for most of the U.S., but if you happen to be on the Florida Keys watch the Crow in late winter: when he is due south you may see far below, just above the sea, the stars of the Cross, provided no cloud banks bar your view at the horizon.

**BEST TIMES** for VIRGIN and CROW: April, May, June.
               SCALES: June and July.
               Calendar Charts 4 to 8.

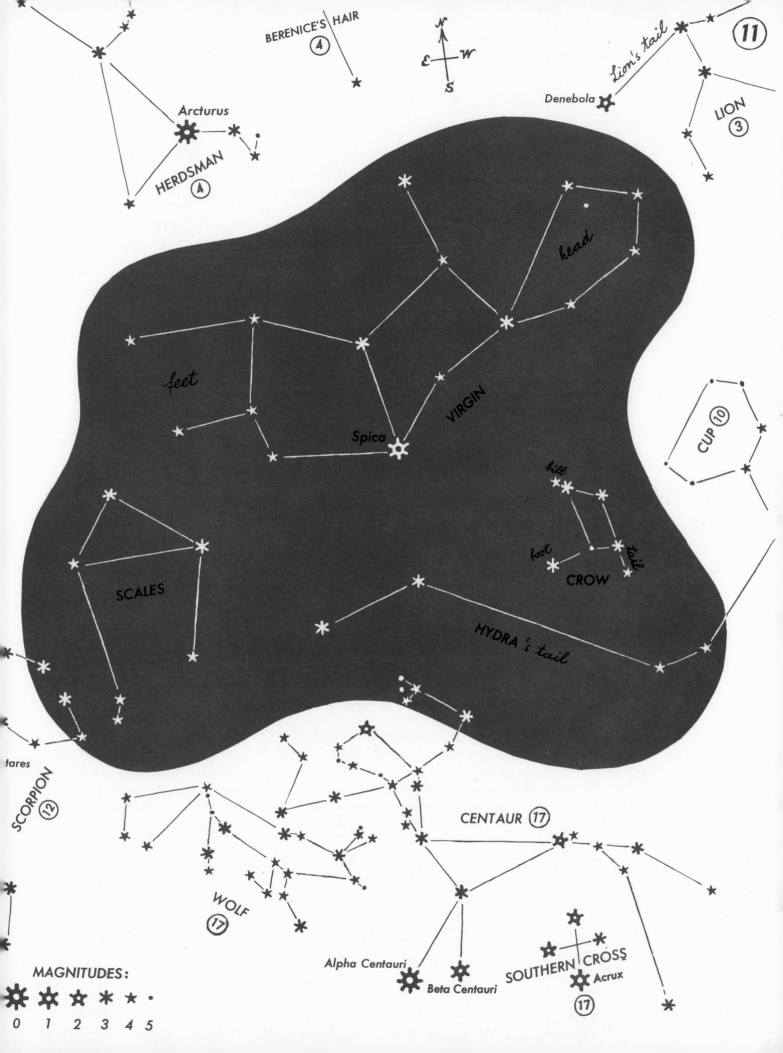

BERENICE'S HAIR
④

Lion's tail

⑪

Denebola

LION
③

N
E   W
S

Arcturus

HERDSMAN
④

head

CUP ⑩

feet

VIRGIN

Spica

bill

SCALES

foot          tail

CROW

HYDRA's tail

tares

SCORPION
⑫

CENTAUR ⑰

WOLF
⑰

Alpha Centauri

Beta Centauri

SOUTHERN CROSS

Acrux

⑰

MAGNITUDES:

0   1   2   3   4   5

## SERPENT HOLDER, SCORPION

**SERPENT HOLDER** (OPHIUCHUS): Vast group, somewhat complex,[1] resembling a voodoo doctor holding the pieces of a snake torn in two. To trace this figure, start with bright star at top of triangular head, left of Hercules' forward foot. The two pairs of stars in the doctor's shoulders are easily recognized. Next trace the huge rectangular body, then the right arm with SERPENT'S front part. The snake's head is a pretty little group, south of the Crown. The left arm with the Serpent's tail comes next, and last the rather dim feet. If you succeed in seeing the whole after a few trials, you feel you have accomplished something.

An odd thing about the Serpent Holder is that it reaches into the zodiac, yet is not by tradition counted among the zodiacal figures, possibly because there would then be 13 constellations instead of 12.

**SCORPION** (SCORPIUS): Beautiful constellation in the zodiac. Unfortunately a little too far south to be seen in all its splendor in the northern United States. It really looks like a scorpion, formed by a number of bright stars. The brightest is brilliant ANTARES, of 1st mag. and distinctly reddish. Antares (Ant-Ares) means rival of Mars, Ares being Greek for Mars. If Antares and the planet Mars are close together, as sometimes happens, they can be confused, because both are red.

Antares is another supergiant, 300 times the sun's diameter and over 3000 times as luminous as our mother star. It would shine even brighter if it were not so far away, almost 300 light-years. Antares is close to the ecliptic and sometimes hidden by the moon, like Regulus, Spica and Aldebaran.

Look for the CAT'S EYES, a close pair of stars in the Scorpion's tail. You will find the name quite fitting.

You can't miss the Scorpion if you use the proper Calendar Chart. Remember that there may be planets nearby. In the middle northern latitudes the constellation is never very high up, and always in the southern part of the sky.

NOTE: To speak of the *Serpent Holder* as a doctor is not a mere whim. The figure is thought to represent *Asklepios*, Greek god of medicine who can be traced back to the Egyptian *Imhotep* (about 2900 B.C.), eminent physician and architect: first man of science in recorded history. The Serpent Holder thus becomes, indirectly, the only constellation representing a historical person.

In Greek mythology, Asklepios was originally a mortal physician who never lost a patient by death. This alarmed Hades, god of the Dead, who feared unemployment, and when Asklepios tried to revive *Orion*, who had been killed by a scorpion, Hades prevailed on his brother Zeus to liquidate Asklepios with a thunderbolt. In recognition of his merits, however, Asklepios was put into the sky as a constellation, together with the scorpion but far away from Orion to avoid further trouble. Since then, Orion and Scorpion never meet, being on opposite sides of the sky. When you see one, you cannot see the other.

**BEST TIMES** for SERPENT HOLDER and SCORPION: July and August.
Calendar Charts 6 to 9.

[1] Technically, it's two constellations: one the *man*, the other the SERPENT (SERPENS) in two separate parts: HEAD (CAPUT) and TAIL (CAUDA).

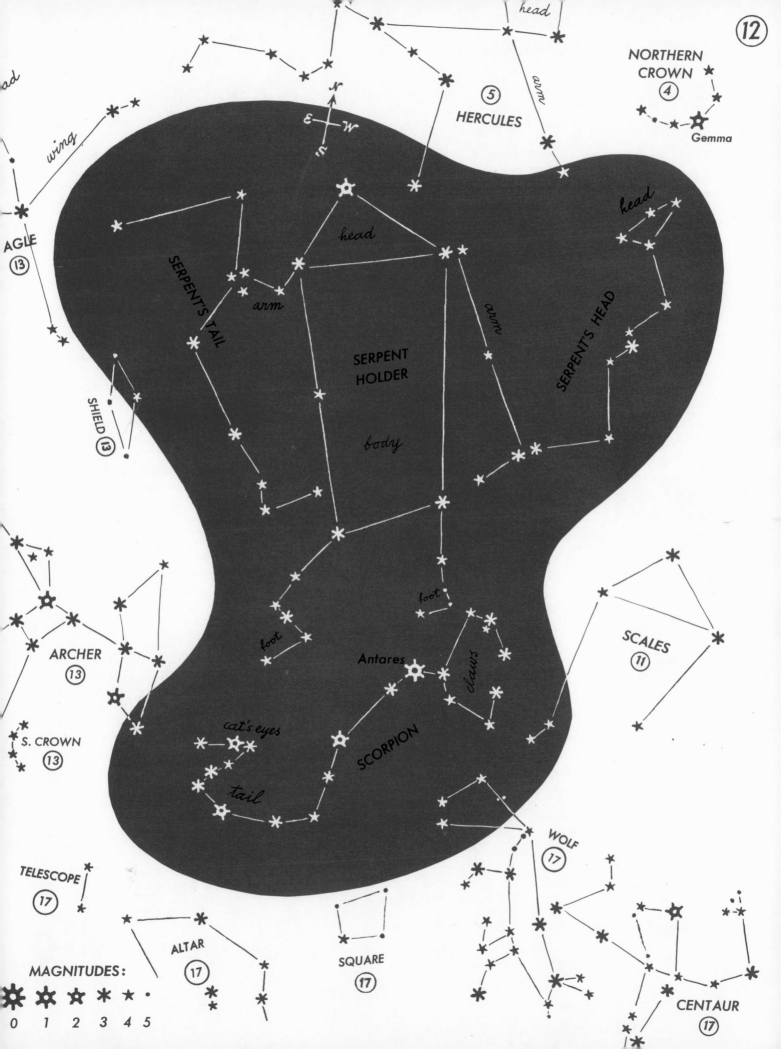

AGLE
13

wing

ad

head

NORTHERN
CROWN
4

12

5 HERCULES

arm

Gemma

N
E W
S

SERPENT'S TAIL

head

arm

head

SERPENT
HOLDER

arm

SERPENT'S HEAD

SHIELD
13

body

foot

foot

SCALES
11

ARCHER
13

Antares

claws

S. CROWN
13

cat's eyes

SCORPION

tail

WOLF
17

TELESCOPE
17

ALTAR
17

SQUARE
17

CENTAUR
17

MAGNITUDES:

0  1  2  3  4  5

## EAGLE, ARCHER, ARROW, DOLPHIN, SOUTHERN CROWN, SHIELD

**EAGLE (AQUILA):** Beautiful constellation; the shape of a great bird soaring with widespread wings is impressive. His head, three stars in a straight row, is a landmark of the sky in summer and early fall, you can hardly miss it. One star in the head is faint, another fairly bright; the middle one is the brightest: yellowish-white ALTAIR (1st mag.), next to Alpha Centauri (chart 17), Sirius, and Procyon our closest neighbor among the brighter stars, only 16 light-years away [1] and coming closer by 1000 miles a minute. Altair, Vega (in the Lyre), and Deneb (in the Swan) form a huge right triangle, known to all navigators; see sketch below. The Eagle is flying toward the Swan; they seem about to meet head-on, both in the Milky Way.

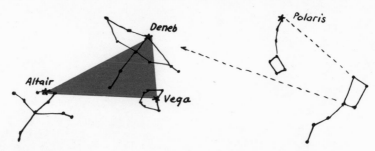

**ARCHER (SAGITTARIUS):** The Eagle's tail points toward this fine constellation. The stars in its lower part are faint and not often seen in our latitudes because of ground haze. Those of the bow and body are brighter. Trace the body first: 4 fairly bright stars forming a small quadrangle (about one-quarter the size of the Big Dipper's bowl). This group is called the MILK DIPPER: it is close to the Milky Way. The Archer's head is adorned with a feather and his bow is pointed toward the Scorpion, apparently with intent to kill—perhaps to avenge Orion's death.

The Archer is partly in the Milky Way and also in the zodiac, so watch out for planets.

**ARROW (SAGITTA):** Small constellation but quite striking for its size. Halfway between the heads of the Swan and the Eagle, in the Milky Way.

**DOLPHIN (DELPHINUS):** Very tiny, with faint stars only, but the stars are so close together that the figure is easily seen on clear, dark nights; it looks charming, swimming just outside the Milky Way, not far from the Eagle's head.

**SOUTHERN CROWN (CORONA AUSTRALIS):** Above our horizon when the Archer is at his highest, but too faint to be seen through the ground haze in middle northern latitudes. It can be seen in the southernmost U.S. but is less impressive than the Northern Crown.

**SHIELD (SCUTUM):** Modern constellation, small and dull.

**BEST TIMES** for EAGLE: July through October.
           ARCHER: July and August.
           ARROW and DOLPHIN: July through November.
           Calendar Charts 7 to 11.

[1] Altair is only 1½ times as large across as the sun, and about 9 times as luminous. We could not see Altair at all if it were as far away as Deneb (500 light-years).

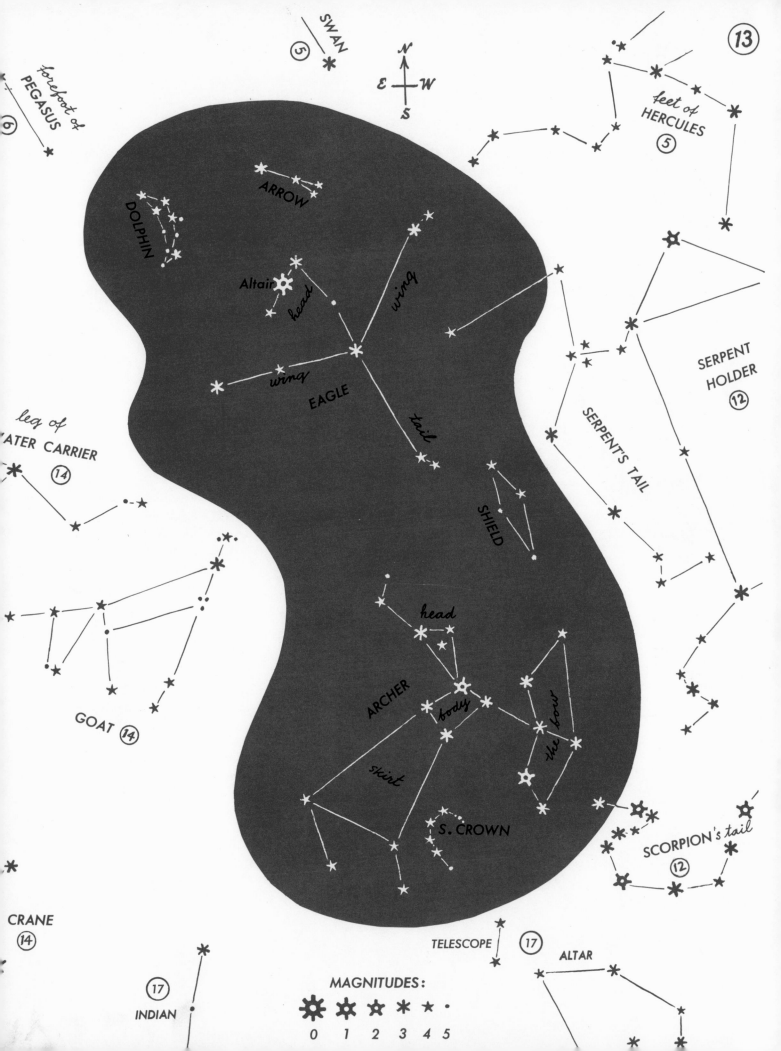

## GOAT, WATER CARRIER, SOUTHERN FISH

**GOAT** (CAPRICORNUS): Faint constellation. If it were not in the zodiac most people would not even know its name. It is in the southern sky and never high up in the northern U.S., which makes it hard to see unless visibility is perfect. The three stars in the Eagle's head point toward the Goat's tail: this part is easiest recognized with its three stars close together. The star at the tip of the horn lies on a straight line from Altair, in the Eagle, to Fomalhaut, in the Southern Fish (see below). If you see a really bright star in the Goat it does not belong to the constellation but is a planet.

**WATER CARRIER** (AQUARIUS): Faint and complicated. Like Crab and Goat, the Water Carrier owes his reputation to being a member of the zodiac. He seems to be running, holding a vessel with his bent arm; two jets of water are flowing from the vessel down to the *Southern Fish*. The small group of stars which mark the man's head are on a line drawn diagonally across the *Great Square,* from Andromeda's head to Pegasus' tail, and beyond. This group is easy to find; the rest of the sprawling figure can be traced from there, but it takes some effort and a very clear, dark night.

**LITTLE HORSE** (EQUULEUS): Barely visible, it is so tiny and faint. Don't bother.

Fomalhaut

**SOUTHERN FISH** (PISCIS AUSTRINUS): The faint stars which make up most of this constellation cannot be seen in our latitudes. They are above the horizon at times but too low to penetrate the ground haze. The constellation's main star, however, is all the more conspicuous: bluish-white FOMALHAUT, one of the 20 brightest stars. You can hardly fail to see it when it is up; a line through the two bright stars on the Pegasus side of the Great Square and far downward points straight to brilliant Fomalhaut, solitary in a very dull region. In case you find another bright star halfway between the Great Square and Fomalhaut, it's not a star but a planet passing through the Water Carrier.

FOMALHAUT is one of our closer neighbors, about 22 light-years away and 13 times as luminous as the sun. It announces the coming of fall: the leaves begin to turn when you see it for the first time at nightfall, in mid or late September.

South of the Southern Fish are the constellations CRANE (GRUS) and PHOENIX. In the northern U.S., both birds just raise their heads above the horizon, and one or two of their brighter stars may be seen SW and SE of Fomalhaut, but in the far south they can be seen whole, under good conditions.

NOTE: Water Carrier and Southern Fish both have to do with *water*. They belong to the group of constellations which make up the "Wet Region" of the sky. Fishes and Whale, on the next chart, and Eridanus River on chart 9, also belong to it. It's a dull region with few bright stars.

**BEST TIMES** for GOAT and WATER CARRIER: August through October.
SOUTHERN FISH: September through November.
Calendar Charts 8 to 11.

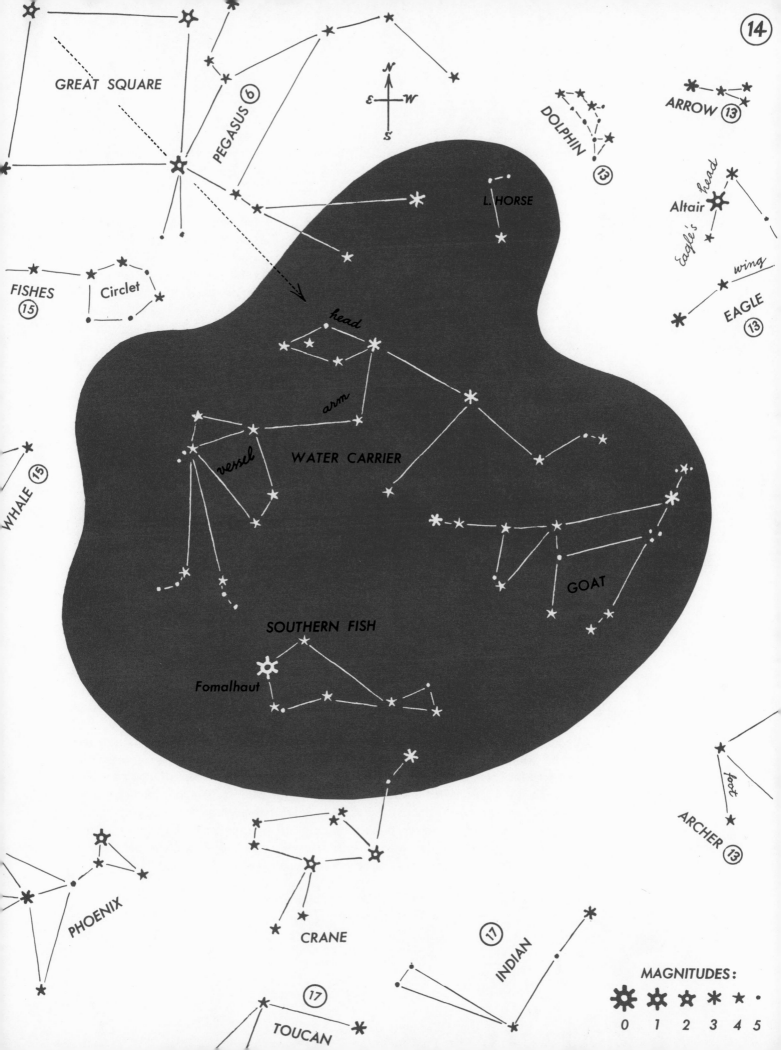

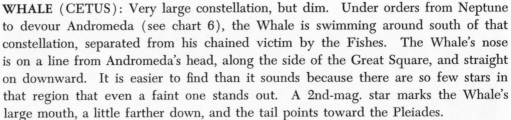

## FISHES, WHALE

**FISHES (PISCES):** Large but faint constellation; next to the Crab the faintest one in the zodiac. (Look for planets!) It looks like two fishes, each one caught on a line, both lines tied together in a knot. The NORTHERN FISH is a small triangle of faint stars just south of Andromeda's hip. The WESTERN FISH or CIRCLET is a little brighter. Its ring-like shape is easily recognized, on clear nights, south of the southern side of the Great Square. To find the KNOT draw a line from Andromeda's brighter foot to the Ram's head and about the same distance beyond.

The V on the chart, to the left of the Circlet, marks the *vernal equinox,* an important point in the sky, on the ecliptic, the sun's yearly path among the stars. When the sun reaches this spot, on or about March 21, night and day are equal (hence *equi*—equal, *nox*—night), and *spring begins* on our hemisphere. More about this on page 119, figure 19. The *zero hour circle* (the sky's "Greenwich line," see page 40) also goes through this point. It is marked roughly by a line from the Pole Star through the last star in Cassiopeia's W, then along the east side of the Great Square, on to the Whale's snout and down to the fairly bright star in the head of Phoenix.

**WHALE (CETUS):** Very large constellation, but dim. Under orders from Neptune to devour Andromeda (see chart 6), the Whale is swimming around south of that constellation, separated from his chained victim by the Fishes. The Whale's nose is on a line from Andromeda's head, along the side of the Great Square, and straight on downward. It is easier to find than it sounds because there are so few stars in that region that even a faint one stands out. A 2nd-mag. star marks the Whale's large mouth, a little farther down, and the tail points toward the Pleiades.

The Whale contains a famous variable star, MIRA (Latin for wonderful). Mira varies in 331 days from 10th mag. (invisible without a telescope) to about 3rd mag. and back, and most of the time you don't see it. The solitary 4th-mag. star below the Whale marks the SCULPTOR, a dim modern constellation; the other stars in this group are too faint to be shown here.

Whale and Fishes are in the "Wet Region" of the sky mentioned on chart 14. Quite fittingly, these constellations are highest around November, a rainy month in many parts of our hemisphere.

The faint star at the corner of the Whale's mouth is TAU CETI, the third nearest star visible to the naked eye in our latitudes; only Sirius and Procyon are nearer. It is about 10 light-years away and only about one-third as luminous as our sun. After having mentioned so many stars brighter than the sun, it seems only fair to point out a star which is dimmer. The brilliant stars are the ones that are talked about, and this creates the impression—an erroneous one—that our sun is a rather poor member of the celestial community. In fact, the sun is a better-than-average star. Among the 20 stars less than 13 light-years away from us, only two are superior to the sun (Sirius and Procyon), one is about the same (Alpha Centauri), and all the others are weaker. This may comfort one's pride as an inhabitant of the solar system.

**BEST TIME** for WHALE and FISHES: October through January.
Calendar Charts 1, 9, 10, 11, and 12.

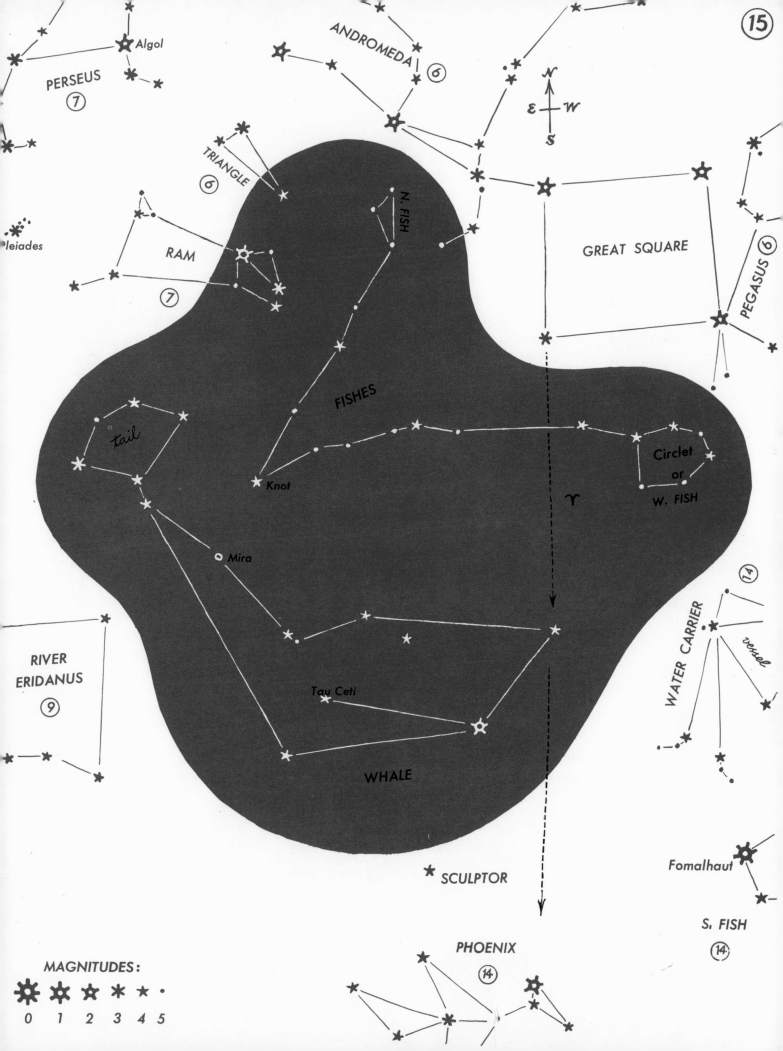

ANDROMEDA ⑥

PERSEUS ⑦

Algol

N. FISH

TRIANGLE ⑥

RAM ⑦

Pleiades

N  
E — W  
S

GREAT SQUARE

PEGASUS ⑥

FISHES

tail

Knot

Circlet or W. FISH

♈

Mira

RIVER ERIDANUS ⑨

Tau Ceti

WHALE

WATER CARRIER ⑭

vessel

SCULPTOR

Fomalhaut

S. FISH ⑭

PHOENIX ⑭

MAGNITUDES:

0  1  2  3  4  5

## SOUTHERNMOST CONSTELLATIONS   I

The constellations shown on charts 16 and 17 lie close to the south pole of the sky. In middle latitudes, around 40° north, most of them are entirely out of sight. The farther south you go, the more they will come into view, and if you pass the equator you will see them all at one time or another. Except for Ship, Centaur, Wolf, and Altar they are of modern origin, and most of them are rather dull. The Calendar Charts on pages 74–97 show you when to see them or, if you are farther south than latitude 25° north, look at Calendar Charts 14–16.

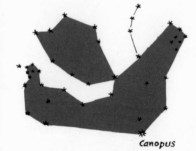

Canopus

**THE SHIP,** a large majestic group, is formed by four constellations: KEEL (CARINA), STERN (PUPPIS), SAIL (VELA),[1] and COMPASS (PYXIS). Originally they were considered as one—the Ship Argo on which, according to Greek myth, Jason and the Argonauts sailed in quest of the Golden Fleece. The Ship is not too hard to trace when high enough in the sky, and is well worth the effort. Its brightest star, CANOPUS, is second only to Sirius in brightness, yellowish white, 100 light-years away, 2000 times as luminous as the sun. You see Canopus very well in the southernmost states and may even get a glimpse of it as far north as Tennessee. Officially the Ship has no bow but the eastern part of the Keel makes a good substitute, figurehead and all. In the stern a small group of stars marks the transom but the ship's Compass looks rather like a tiller. As the Ship moves across the sky from east to west it is sailing backwards, as though it were trying to correct an error of navigation. The group of four stars joined by dotted lines very much resembles, and is often mistaken for, the Southern Cross nearby, and is aptly called the FALSE CROSS.

The lesser constellations in these parts include two fishes: FLYING FISH (VOLANS) and SWORDFISH (DORADO); one bird: DOVE (COLUMBA); one reptile: HYDRUS, the male water snake, supposedly mate of Hydra, which is female; and four objects: EASEL (PICTOR),[1] NET (RETICULUM), diamond-shaped, a bit small for the Swordfish near it; CLOCK (HOROLOGIUM); and FURNACE (FORNAX) with just one 4th-mag. star. More interesting is the 1st-mag. star at the bottom of the chart: ACHERNAR, brilliant bluish, at the southern end of the RIVER ERIDANUS, 70 light-years away and 200 times as luminous as the sun. At the proper times it can be seen from the southernmost states.

A special feature of this region are the two MAGELLANIC CLOUDS, the LARGER and the SMALLER, named after the great Portuguese sailor Magellan. Faint silvery patches on the dark sky, they look like stray parts of the Milky Way. They are galaxies composed of millions of stars, satellites of our own Milky Way galaxy (see page 145), and small as galaxies go: about 30,000 and 22,000 light-years across and about 140,000 and 160,000 light-years away. To see them well you have to cross the equator although they rise above the horizon at about 15° latitude north.

[1] Vela is plural, the Sails, but the name designates just one constellation, shaped like one sail only, so it seems sensible to use the singular form in English. Pictor is Latin for Painter; this group was originally called Equuleus Pictoris, Painter's Easel, and this name, or just Easel for short, goes better with the triangular shape of the group.

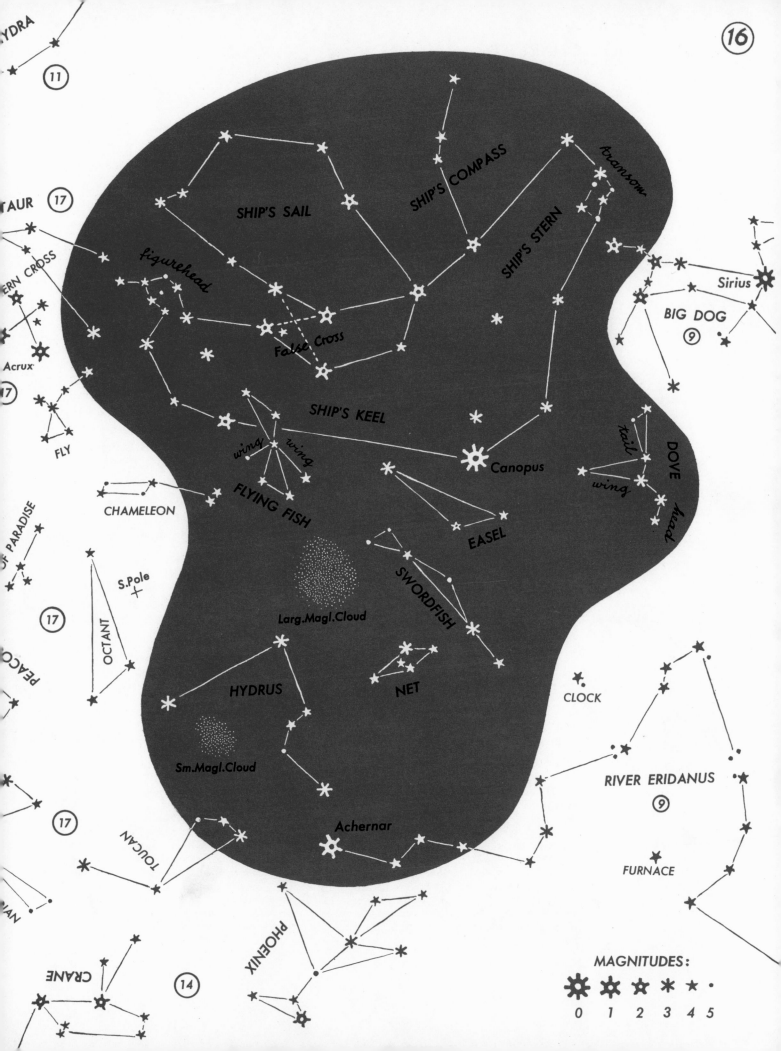

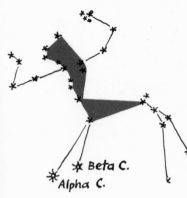

## SOUTHERNMOST CONSTELLATIONS  II

**CENTAUR (CENTAURUS):** Large impressive figure, not as hard to trace as you might conclude from its complex shape.  Half horse, half man, the Centaur is held to represent Chiron, the teacher of Jason of Argonaut fame.  Two 1st-mag. stars mark his forefeet: ALPHA CENTAURI,[1] brighter of the two, yellow-orange, is the nearest of all bright stars, only 4.3 light-years away from the solar system.  It's actually a double star, two stars revolving around each other, the larger one about the size of the sun and slightly more luminous.  BETA CENTAURI, bluish and not quite as brilliant as Alpha, is 190 light-years away and 1500 times as luminous as the sun.  To us Alpha appears brighter because it is so much closer.

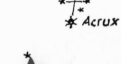

**SOUTHERN CROSS (CRUX):** Small[2] but famous.  Its longer bar points almost exactly toward the south pole of the sky which, alas, is not marked by any bright star like its northern counterpart.  Beware of the False Cross (page 60) which is larger, less bright, and does not point south.  The bluish 1st-mag. star in the Cross, commonly called ACRUX,[1] shows up as a double, even in small telescopes; the pair is about 220 light-years away and, combined, about 1400 times as luminous as the sun.  Crux is Latin for Cross, without Southern, for there is no constellation Northern Cross; the group in the Swan so named (page 38) lacks official standing.  But Southern Cross sounds romantic, and the name is popular, so why not keep it.  Northern visitors, though, are often disappointed at the sight: it is not as grand as they expected and looks more like a kite than a cross.  Still, it's a graceful group.

Only two of the other constellations in this region have stars as bright as 2nd mag.: the PEACOCK (PAVO), marked by a square body and triangular tail; and the SOUTHERN TRIANGLE (TRIANGULUM AUSTRALE), brighter and larger than its northern namesake.  The WOLF (LUPUS), quite wolf-like in shape, trots beneath one arm of the Centaur, who seems about to seize him; none of his stars is brighter than 3rd mag.  The FLY (MUSCA), busy little group near the Cross, is the only insect in the sky.  The dull OCTANT (OCTANS) contains the starless south pole of the sky within its area though not within the shape shown here.  Near the Triangle lie two draftsman's tools: the DIVIDERS (CIRCINUS) and the SQUARE (NORMA).  The BIRD OF PARADISE has none of the splendor of his earthly cousin.  A close pair of stars, easy to spot, marks the head of the CHAMELEON.  The TOUCAN (TUCANA) should have a prominent beak, and he has.  The INDIAN (INDUS) looks faintly like a tomahawk.  Don't bother about the TELESCOPE (TELESCOPIUM), two 4th-mag. stars near the ALTAR, an irregular pentagon with two stars inside marking the altar's flame.

[1] The small letters of the Greek alphabet followed by the constellation's Latin name in the genitive are used in astronomy to mark the stars in a constellation, roughly in order of brightness.  Besides, many bright stars have proper names: Alpha ($\alpha$) Leonis (gen. of Leo, Lion) is named Regulus, Beta ($\beta$) Cygni (gen. of Cygnus, Swan) is called Albireo, and so on.  The proper names of the Centaur's brightest stars, however (HADAR and WAZN), are no longer used.  Instead they are plainly called Alpha and Beta Centauri (gen. of Centaurus) but in navigation Alpha is known as Rigil Kentaurus.  The brightest star in the Cross is widely but not officially called ACRUX, a contraction of sorts of Alpha Crucis.

[2] In fact, the Cross is the smallest, in area, of all constellations.  If other constellations appear smaller on these charts they do so because they have fewer bright stars.  The borderlines of the constellations, which determine their areas, are not given in these charts; you find them in any star atlas.

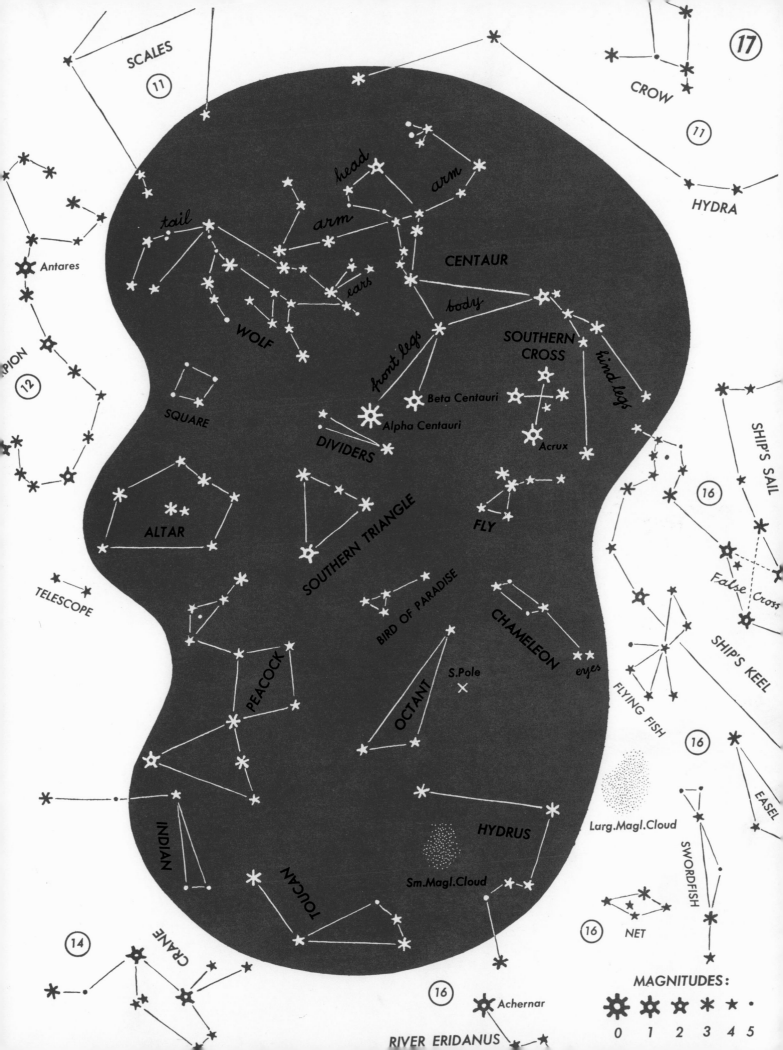

# PART 3

# THE STARS THROUGH THE YEAR

PART THREE

# THE STARS THROUGH THE YEAR

THE twelve CALENDAR CHARTS on pages 74 to 97 show *where* to look for a constellation and *when* to look for it at different hours of the night, at all times of the year, any year, and from any place, between latitudes 25° and 55° north. Farther north, use chart 13; farther south; charts 14–16.

We cannot do with one single chart because the sky is always changing, slowly but continuously, as the stars revolve around the pole. Watch the sky off and on for a few hours one night, and you will see the change. Stars you saw in the west an hour ago have set; stars which were high up are lower now and have wandered westward; stars you saw low above the eastern horizon have climbed higher, and new stars have risen in the east. This goes on and on, without end.

And the sky changes not only from hour to hour. It also changes from night to night, week to week, month to month, season to season. The sky on a January evening looks different from the one on an April or July or October evening.

Why? Because of *four minutes*. The revolution of the stars round the pole does not take a full 24 hours but only about 23 hours 56 minutes: about four minutes less than a day. The stars therefore rise *four minutes earlier every day* than the day before.[1]

If it were not for these four minutes, if the stars took *exactly* twenty-four hours to make one complete turn, we should see the stars in exactly the same position at the same hour every night, and stargazing would be the simplest thing in the world.

---

[1] Let us here consider merely the *fact* (which you can observe for yourself) and its consequences. For explanation see page 122.

Now four minutes a day does not sound like much but it adds up. In a month it makes 30 × 4 minutes = 2 full hours. One month from today the stars will rise two hours earlier than today. *One month later—two hours earlier* is the simple formula on which the whole star schedule is based.

Two hours a month makes twenty-four hours in a year, therefore after a year the whole cycle repeats itself in exactly the same fashion. On November 12, 9 P.M. this year, for instance, you see the stars in the same position as you saw them on November 12, 9 P.M. of last year, and as you will see them at 9 P.M. on November 12 next year.

Let us follow a star through the year. Suppose on April 7 it rises at 9 P.M. and sets at 4 A.M. the same night. This would be its schedule:

April 7: rises 9 P.M.; sets 4 A.M. You can see it all night.
May 7: rises 7 P.M. (daylight!); sets 2 A.M.
June 7: rises 5 P.M.; sets at midnight. You can see it only for a few hours.
July 7: rises 3 P.M.; sets 10 P.M. You barely get a glimpse of it.

The star is now out of step with the night:
August 7: rises at 1 P.M., sets at 8 P.M.:
September 7: rises at 11 A.M., sets at 6 P.M.:
October 7: rises at 9 A.M., sets at 4 P.M.:  } all daylight hours. You can't see it at all.
November 7: rises at 7 A.M., sets at 2 P.M.:

As the star continues to rise 4 minutes earlier from day to day, it slowly gets back into step again with the night:
December 7: rises at 5 A.M., sets at 12 NOON: you see it just before dawn.
January 7: rises 3 A.M., sets 10 A.M.: you can see it for a few hours if you care to.
February 7: rises at 1 A.M., sets at 8 A.M.
March 7: rises at 11 P.M.—not too inconvenient an hour—and sets at 6 A.M., and on
April 7: rises at 9 P.M., sets at 4 A.M.: we are back where we started.

As you see, this star gives its best showing in spring—March, April, May—and we should call it a typical *Spring Star.* By the same token, we speak of *Summer, Fall,* and *Winter Stars,* or spring, summer, fall, and winter skies.[1]

To call a star a Spring Star does not necessarily mean you cannot see it in other seasons also. You might, but perhaps not at convenient hours. If you are impatient

[1] The sky is more splendid in winter than in other seasons, partly because cold air is normally dryer, hence clearer, than warmer air; but the main reason is that on winter evenings the richest region of the sky is in full view. The stars are unevenly scattered over the firmament: some regions are rich in stars, some outright poor.

you can see the Spring Stars in midwinter. All you have to do is go out, say, at 3 in the morning in late January instead of 11 at night in late March, or 9 in the evening in late April.

*Ah — Spring Stars!*

TIME TABLE: The changes of the sky from month to month through the year (or, for that matter, for intervals of two hours in a single night) are shown on the twelve Calendar Charts on pages 74–97. The *Time Table* on page 73[1] tells you at a glance which chart to use. This depends on the hour as well as on the date. For instance, if it is January 15 and you are watching the stars at 8 P.M., the time table tells you to use chart 1; if at 10 P.M., chart 2; if at midnight, chart 3. Time passes fast with stargazing, and during the same night you may have to use several charts.

THE CHARTS AND HOW TO USE THEM: The charts on pages 74–97 are double: the left-hand charts show the stars the way you see them in the sky; the right-hand charts show the same stars connected by lines to form the constellations. Before you go out look at the constellations on the right-hand charts, then try to find them on the left-hand ones. Do this whenever you have time. It may be puzzling at first but it makes excellent practice for the real sky. Besides, it's fun, and weather is no problem. What stars you see when you are outdoors depends not only on date and hour but also, to an extent, on your latitude. Therefore, the charts are drawn with three overlapping horizons, marked lat. 30°, 40°, and 50°. Thus they will be equally useful in different parts of our vast country—say, in St. Augustine, Florida (lat. about 30°), or Columbus, Ohio (lat. 40°), or Blaine, Montana (lat. 50°). Choose

[1] This time table applies only to charts 1–12. Charts 13–16, which show only four aspects of the sky for each group of latitudes, contain time tables of their own.

the horizon nearest your latitude, on the chart you have picked from the time table; inside this horizon you find the stars you can see at that moment while the stars outside it are below your horizon and you won't see them.

As you glance through the charts you will notice that by far the greater part of the sky is the same at all three latitudes. It is mainly the southernmost and northernmost parts of the sky that differ: in the southernmost part of the sky the southern observer sees stars the observer farther north does not see, and vice versa. On chart 2, for instance, the bright star Canopus in the south is visible at lat. 30° but not at lat. 40° or 50°, while in the northern part of the sky the star Deneb is visible at lat. 50° but not at lat. 40° or 30°. You will also see that the Pole Star is much nearer the horizon (that is, lower in the sky) at lat. 30° than at 40° or 50°. The farther south you are, the lower in the sky the Pole Star will be; the farther north, the higher.

Some stars and constellations appear on the white of the page, beyond the horizon. This makes the charts useful at least as far south as lat. 25° (e.g., southern Florida) and as far north as lat. 55° (southern Alaska). If you are farther north than lat. 55° or farther south than lat. 25°, use the additional charts 13–16 on pages 98–105.

And now let us go outdoors: Find *north* first by spotting the Pole Star from the Big Dipper. The stars in the north, circling around the Pole Star, are the same throughout the year, and you will soon know them at sight. Then look *west* (because the western stars are setting; if you wait till you have scanned the rest of the sky some of them will be gone), then south and east. As you look west, east, north, or south, always turn the book so that the words "west," "east," "north," or "south" on the chart read right side up. By doing so, you will see the constellations on the chart in the same position as you see them in the sky. Look for the *brightest stars* first (they are mentioned at the bottom of each chart), then for the most conspicuous *constellations*, and then for the fainter ones. If you want details about a constellation you are looking at, the *number near its name* tells you at a glance on which constellation chart to find it. To examine the stars overhead, better sit or lie down; it's a rewarding experience. A blanket or chair will come in handy. If you stand up and crane your neck you soon get dizzy, and your muscles will ache the next morning. Don't try too hard when a constellation is very low above the horizon: the atmosphere near the ground is denser than high up, and a ground haze usually blots out all fainter stars,[1] even on clear nights, and makes the brighter ones look dimmer.

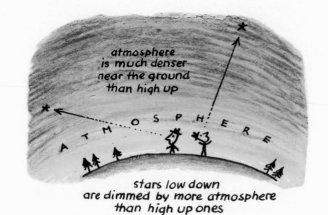

Figure 9: Effect of the Atmosphere

A FEW THINGS TO BE AWARE OF: Sun and moon look much larger near the horizon than when they are high up (the so-called Moon Illusion[2]), and the same is true of the constellations. They seem to shrink as they rise. Just watch, say, Cassiopeia at nightfall in August, low in the sky: it looks quite large; at midnight, about halfway up in the sky, it will look smaller, and even smaller before dawn when it is almost overhead. By the same token, stars in the lower part of the sky seem higher up than they actually turn out to be if we measure their height, or altitude. The Pole Star, e.g., which at lat. 40° is about 40° above the horizon (which means 10° closer to the horizon than to the zenith), seems to be at least halfway up in the sky.

Many a novice stargazer is surprised at the acrobatics the constellations seem to perform in the sky. Just as the Dipper on the umbrella (page 22) may be upside down or sideways, so the figures in the real sky will appear in varied positions. Leaf through the calendar charts and follow the course of one constellation: the Virgin, e.g., on

[1] Nevertheless, the fainter stars near the horizon are shown on the charts. They gradually become visible as they rise, and it helps in tracing a constellation if you know where those stars are, even before you actually see them. The same goes, vice versa, for faint stars which are setting.

[2] It actually *is* an illusion. When measured or photographed the moon has exactly the same size, whether high or low in the sky. We have more experience in judging the size of objects (an acquired ability) when looking ahead than when looking straight up, and things seen high overhead (not only the moon) look smaller to us than when seen at the same distance horizontally.

charts 2–8, rises head first, then comes to lie on her back, and goes down feet in the air; or the Twins, on charts 11, 12, and 1–5 (chart 1 being the follow-up to chart 12 in the endless circle of seasons). Such antics result from the sky's rotation around its tilted axis; once you are aware of that they won't confuse you.

Another thing: all stars as we see them in the sky look the same size. Whether we see them with the naked eye or with field glasses or telescopes, they are mere pinpoints of light; the difference is in the *brightness* only: some are brilliant, some dim. On charts, we have to use symbols of *different size* to indicate the different brightnesses, but even the smallest of the symbols is much larger, in proportion, than the brightest star we see in the sky. The effect is that on charts the stars seem to be much closer together, comparatively, than in the sky. Look at Orion's belt, or at the three stars in the Eagle's head, and the difference becomes obvious.

PLANETS: If you find a brilliant star in the sky which is not on the chart it's probably a *planet*. Planets are banned from star charts because they have no fixed residence: they wander around among the constellations.

Of the sun's nine planets (including the earth), five can be seen in the sky with the naked eye: Mercury, Venus, Mars, Jupiter, Saturn. Mercury is so close to the sun that you will hardly ever see it. Of the other four, however, one is usually around, often two, sometimes three—though not necessarily at the same hour—and occasionally all four.

Fortunately the planets always travel along a known path, through the constellations of the *zodiac*, and never stray far from the *ecliptic*. For this reason the ecliptic is shown as a white dotted line on all Calendar Charts. So always watch out for uncharted bright stars near that line: they are probably planets.

VENUS is the brightest of the planets and far outshines all true stars. This makes her easy to detect. Besides, she is never very high up; she either shines above the western horizon after sunset as the *evening star* or above the eastern horizon as the *morning star*. Never look for Venus in the middle of the night. Not quite as brilliant but also brighter than all true stars is JUPITER. He can be high or low, east, south, or west, at any time of the night, anywhere near the ecliptic, and the same goes for MARS and SATURN. Saturn never gets as bright as Jupiter but is always of 1st mag. Mars, however, varies greatly, depending on its distance from the earth:[1] often brighter than Saturn, at rare times as bright as Jupiter or even brighter, it often dims down to 2nd mag.; but brighter or dimmer, you can always tell Mars by its reddish color, and all the planets by their steady light; they twinkle less than the true stars.

The novice stargazer might think planets are a nuisance because of their vaga-bondism, yet spotting the planets is fun if one knows in what constellation they are at the moment. The *Planetary Tables* on pages 134–135 supply this information. Additional data—size, distance, periods of revolution—are to be found on pages 132–133.

THE MILKY WAY appears on the charts as an irregular band, composed of tiny white stipples. Don't look for it in the sky unless the night is clear and dark. A bright moon or a haze, even slight, will blot it out completely, and you rarely see it in big cities with their smog and glare. But when you see it, it not only enhances the splendor of the firmament but also helps you spot the constellations which are on or near it. More about the Milky Way, or *Galaxy*, on page 143.

Finally you may ask: can I use these charts in the western hemisphere only, or in the eastern as well? The answer is, You can use them everywhere: it makes no difference how far east or west you are; only the latitude matters. You can use the same charts and the same time table in Washington, D. C., or Naples, Italy, or Tokyo, Japan. The stars will be the same, at the same hours, by the standard time of those places.

And now, happy stargazing!

---

[1] The distance of Mars from the earth varies much more, in proportion, than that of the other planets: from 34 million miles at its closest, hence brightest, to 247 million miles at its farthest (a factor of more than 7), while Jupiter's distance varies only between 367 and 600 million miles, and Saturn's between 745 and about 1000 million miles.

# TIME TABLE

## FOR SELECTING THE PROPER CALENDAR CHART

Numbers in blue field indicate which chart to use at
any hour of the night, at any date, in any year.

Note: In the rows MAY 1 through JULY 16, the two leftmost columns (5–6 pm, 6–7 pm) are labeled vertically "NO STARS VISIBLE" and "DAYLIGHT OR TWILIGHT"; the two rightmost data columns (5–6 am, 6–7 am) are labeled "DAYLIGHT OR TWILIGHT" and "NO STARS VISIBLE."

| Date | 5–6 pm | 6–7 pm | 7–8 pm | 8–9 pm | 9–10 pm | 10–11 pm | 11–12 midn. | 12–1 | 1–2 am | 2–3 am | 3–4 am | 4–5 am | 5–6 am | 6–7 am | Date |
|---|---|---|---|---|---|---|---|---|---|---|---|---|---|---|---|
| JAN 1 | 11 | 11 | 12 | 12 | 1 | 1 | 2 | 2 | 3 | 3 | 4 | 4 | 5 | 5 | JAN 1 |
| JAN 16 | 11 | 12 | 12 | 1 | 1 | 2 | 2 | 3 | 3 | 4 | 4 | 5 | 5 | 6 | JAN 16 |
| FEB 1 | 12 | 12 | 1 | 1 | 2 | 2 | 3 | 3 | 4 | 4 | 5 | 5 | 6 | 6 | FEB 1 |
| FEB 15 | | 1 | 1 | 2 | 2 | 3 | 3 | 4 | 4 | 5 | 5 | 6 | 6 | | FEB 15 |
| MAR 1 | | 1 | 2 | 2 | 3 | 3 | 4 | 4 | 5 | 5 | 6 | 6 | 7 | | MAR 1 |
| MAR 16 | | | 2 | 3 | 3 | 4 | 4 | 5 | 5 | 6 | 6 | 7 | 7 | | MAR 16 |
| APR 1 | | | 3 | 3 | 4 | 4 | 5 | 5 | 6 | 6 | 7 | 7 | | | APR 1 |
| APR 16 | | | 3 | 4 | 4 | 5 | 5 | 6 | 6 | 7 | 7 | 8 | | | APR 16 |
| MAY 1 | | | | 4 | 5 | 5 | 6 | 6 | 7 | 7 | 8 | 8 | | | MAY 1 |
| MAY 16 | NO STARS VISIBLE | DAYLIGHT OR TWILIGHT | | | 5 | 5 | 6 | 6 | 7 | 7 | 8 | 8 | DAYLIGHT OR TWILIGHT | NO STARS VISIBLE | MAY 16 |
| JUNE 1 | | | | | 5 | 6 | 6 | 7 | 7 | 8 | 8 | 9 | | | JUNE 1 |
| JUNE 16 | | | | | 6 | 6 | 7 | 7 | 8 | 8 | 9 | 9 | | | JUNE 16 |
| JULY 1 | | | | | 6 | 7 | 7 | 8 | 8 | 9 | 9 | 10 | | | JULY 1 |
| JULY 16 | | | 6 | 7 | 7 | 8 | 8 | 9 | 9 | 10 | 10 | | | | JULY 16 |
| AUG 1 | | | 7 | 7 | 8 | 8 | 9 | 9 | 10 | 10 | 11 | | | | AUG 1 |
| AUG 16 | | | 7 | 8 | 8 | 9 | 9 | 10 | 10 | 11 | 11 | 12 | | | AUG 16 |
| SEPT 1 | | | 8 | 8 | 9 | 9 | 10 | 10 | 11 | 11 | 12 | 12 | | | SEPT 1 |
| SEPT 16 | | 8 | 8 | 9 | 9 | 10 | 10 | 11 | 11 | 12 | 12 | 1 | | | SEPT 16 |
| OCT 1 | | 8 | 9 | 9 | 10 | 10 | 11 | 11 | 12 | 12 | 1 | 1 | 2 | | OCT 1 |
| OCT 16 | | 9 | 9 | 10 | 10 | 11 | 11 | 12 | 12 | 1 | 1 | 2 | 2 | | OCT 16 |
| NOV 1 | 9 | 9 | 10 | 10 | 11 | 11 | 12 | 12 | 1 | 1 | 2 | 2 | 3 | | NOV 1 |
| NOV 16 | 9 | 10 | 10 | 11 | 11 | 12 | 12 | 1 | 1 | 2 | 2 | 3 | 3 | 4 | NOV 16 |
| DEC 1 | 10 | 10 | 11 | 11 | 12 | 12 | 1 | 1 | 2 | 2 | 3 | 3 | 4 | 4 | DEC 1 |
| DEC 16 | 10 | 11 | 11 | 12 | 12 | 1 | 1 | 2 | 2 | 3 | 3 | 4 | 4 | 5 | DEC 16 |
| | 5–6 pm | 6–7 pm | 7–8 pm | 8–9 pm | 9–10 pm | 10–11 pm | 11–12 midn. | 12–1 | 1–2 am | 2–3 am | 3–4 am | 4–5 am | 5–6 am | 6–7 am | |

All hours are Standard Time. If you have Daylight Saving Time subtract one
hour. At 11 pm D.S.T., look for 10 pm on Time Table.
On intermediate dates use nearest date on Time Table. For example, on April 24,
9:45 pm, look for May 1; chart to use, between 9 and 10 pm, is #5.

NOTE: The blue fields on this table mark the length of night at latitude 40° north. At
lat. 50°, the longest days and longest nights are longer, and at lat. 30° they are shorter,
by about one hour, than at lat. 40°. For charts 13–16, on pages 98–105, use the time
tables you find on those spreads.

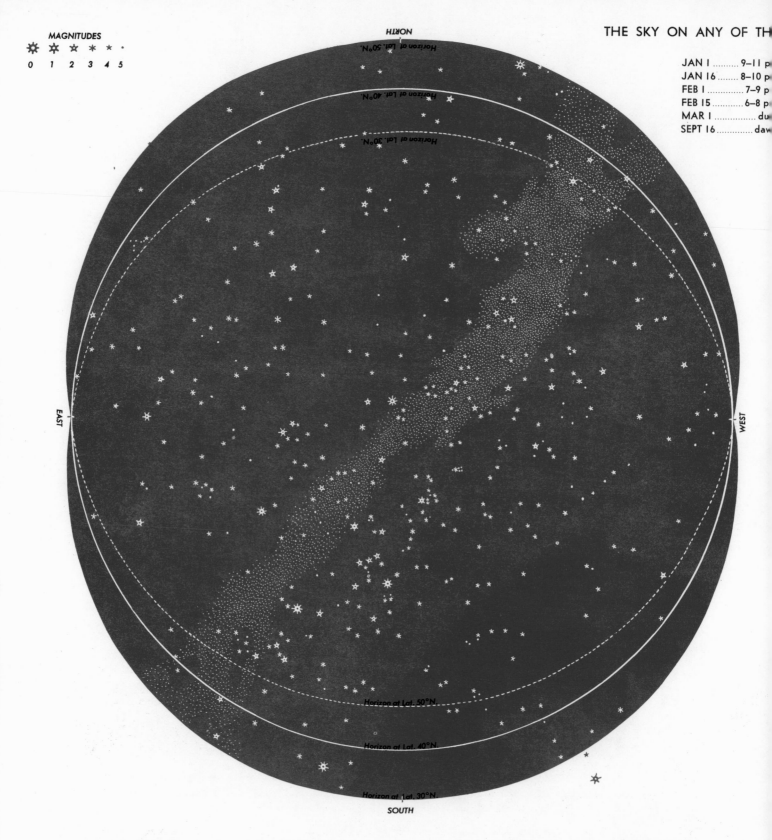

JAN I .......... 9–11 p
JAN 16 .......... 8–10 p
FEB I .............. 7–9 p
FEB 15 .......... 6–8 p
MAR I ................ du
SEPT 16 ............ daw

MAGNITUDES

0   1   2   3   4   5

NORTH

Horizon at Lat. 50°N.

Horizon at Lat. 40°N.

Horizon at Lat. 30°N.

EAST

WEST

Horizon at Lat. 50°N.

Horizon at Lat. 40°N.

Horizon at Lat. 30°N.

SOUTH

Nine 1st-mag. stars are visible at lat. 40°. In order of brightness: **Sirius** in Big Dog, brightest of all stars, bluish, southeast, first star you see at nightfall (except possibly for planets, near ecliptic; check tables pages 134–135); **Capella** in Charioteer, yellowish, overhead; **Rigel** in Orion, bluish white, west of south; **Procyon** in Little Dog, yellow-white, southwest; **Betelgeuse** in Orion, reddish, west of south; **Aldebaran** in Bull, orange, high south; **Pollux**, in Twins, yellowish, high southeast; **Deneb** in Swan, white, setting northwest; **Regulus** in Lion, bluish white, east, going up. At lat. 50°: last glimpse of **Vega** in Lyre, setting west of north. At lat. 35° and farther south: **Canopus** in Ship's

74

OCT 1 ............. 3–5 am
OCT 16 ......... 2–4 am
NOV 1 ............ 1–3 am
NOV 16 .... midn–2 am
DEC 1 ...... 11 pm–1 am
DEC 16 .... 10 pm–midn

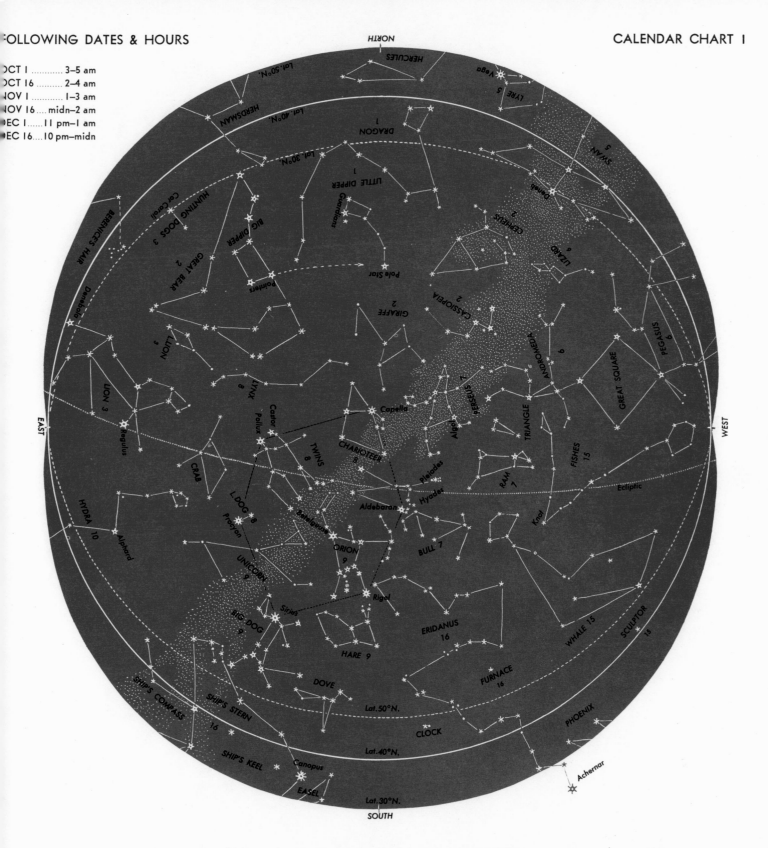

Keel, second brightest of all stars, rising east of south. **Great Square** setting in west; above it, look for **Andromeda Nebula** if the night is clear and dark. **Hare**, below Orion, in good position. Sit down, facing south, to trace the Bull, with **Pleiades** to the right (you can't miss those) and Aldebaran with the **Hyades**; the rest is not so easy but worth the effort. Look for the **Great Hexagon**, outlined on chart, formed by seven 1st-mag. stars: Capella, Pollux, Procyon, Sirius, Rigel, Aldebaran at the corners and Betelgeuse inside. This is the rich region that gives the winter sky its splendor; the region west of it is rather dull, the "Wet Region" with River Eridanus, Whale and Fishes, all going down; you won't see them again till autumn.

FEB 1 .......... 9–11
FEB 15 ........ 8–10
MAR 1 .......... 7–9
MAR 16 ............... d
OCT 1 ............... da
OCT 16 ........ 4–6

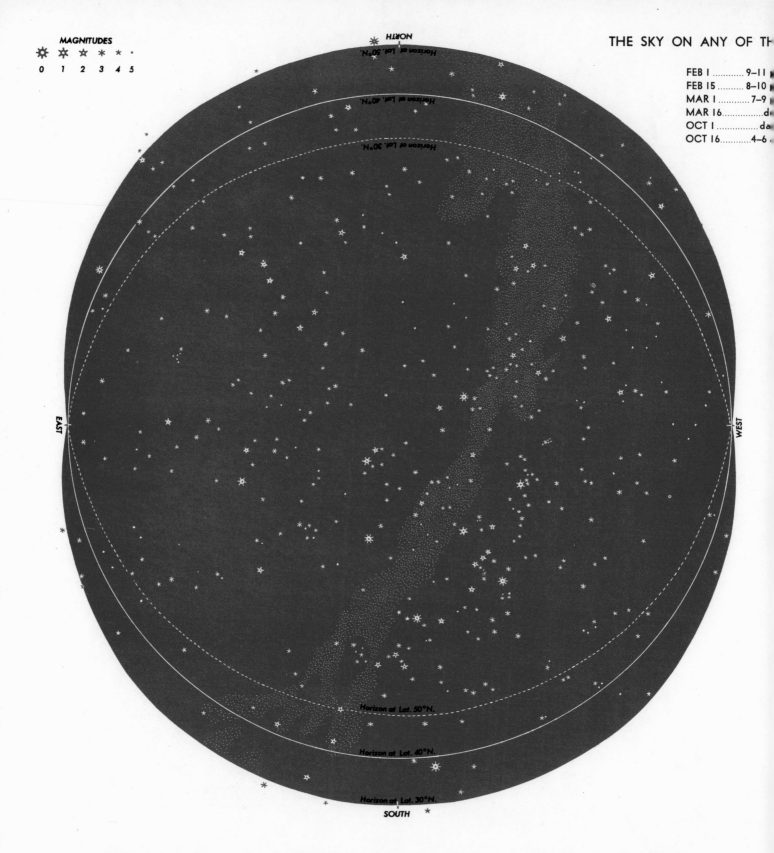

MAGNITUDES

0  1  2  3  4  5

NORTH

Horizon at Lat. 50°N.

Horizon at Lat. 40°N.

Horizon at Lat. 30°N.

EAST

WEST

Horizon at Lat. 50°N.

Horizon at Lat. 40°N.

Horizon at Lat. 30°N.

SOUTH

Eight 1st-mag. stars are visible at lat. 40°. In order of brightness: **Sirius** in Big Dog, bluish, brightest by far, first star you see at nightfall (except possibly for *planets*, near ecliptic; check tables pages 134–135) high above southern horizon; **Capella,** in Charioteer, yellowish, overhead; **Rigel** in Orion, bluish white, west of south; **Procyon** in Little Dog, yellow-white, high in southeast; **Betelgeuse** in Orion, reddish, southwest; **Aldebaran** in Bull, orange, high west of south; **Pollux** in Twins, yellowish, overhead; **Regulus** in Lion, bluish white, south of east. South of lat. 35°: **Canopus** in Ship's Keel,

76

OV 1 ...........3–5 am
OV 16 ..........2–4 am
EC 1 .............1–3 am
EC 16......midn–2 am
AN 1......11 pm–1 am
AN 16....10 pm–midn

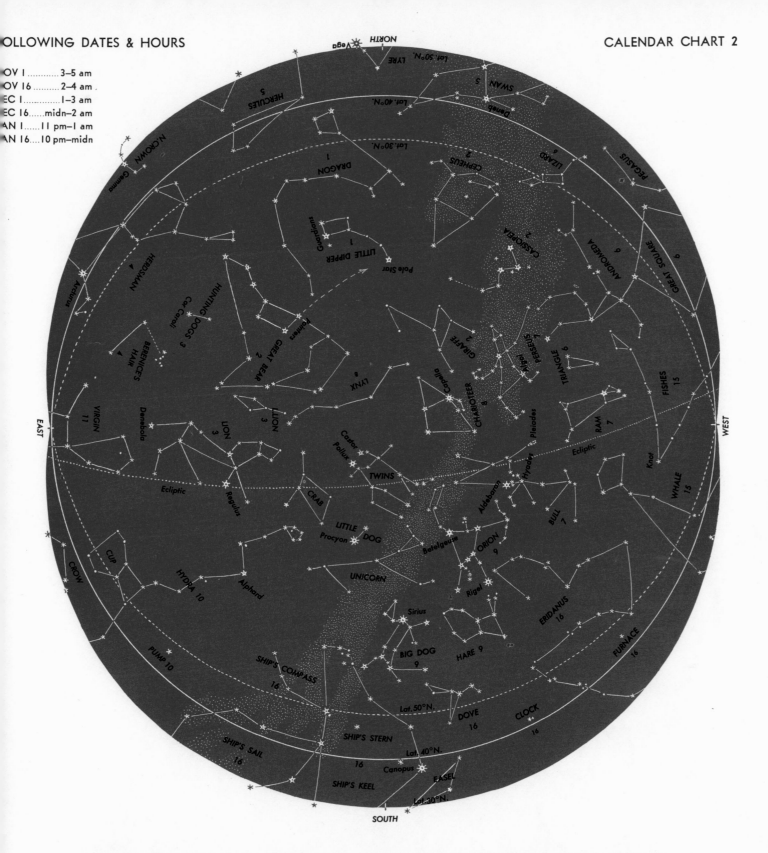

second brightest of all stars, white, low above horizon in south.  Watch horizon north of east for rising **Arcturus** in Herdsman, orange, already farther up if you are farther north than lat. 40°.  Trace the **Great Hexagon,** formed by seven of the twenty brightest stars of the sky (see preceding chart) in richest region of sky; regions to east and west rather dull by contrast.  Look for charming **Pleiades** high east.  Twins almost overhead: sit down, facing south, to see them well.  If you are far south, trace part of the great Ship, and perhaps the Dove, west of Big Dog's hind feet, and, just for sport, the faint Unicorn.

77

MAR 1 .......... 9–11 pm
MAR 16 ......... 8–10 pm
APR 1 ............ 7–9 pm
APR 16 ............. dusk
NOV 1 ............. dawn
NOV 16 ........ 4–6 am

**MAGNITUDES**

0   1   2   3   4   5

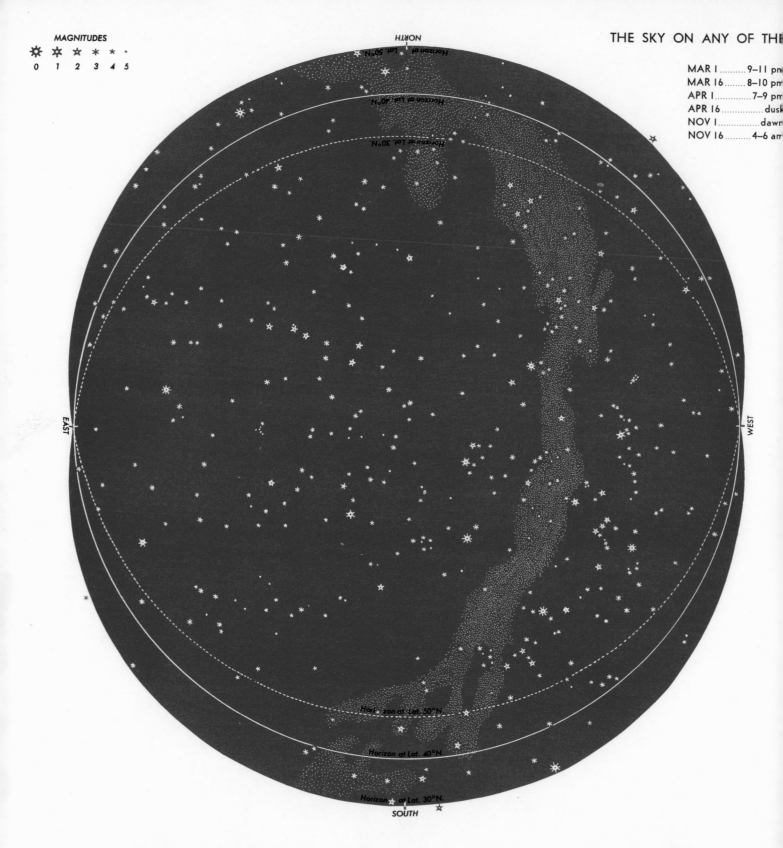

Ten 1st-mag. stars are visible at lat. 40°.  In order of brightness: **Sirius** in Big Dog, bluish, brightest of all stars, southwest, first star you see at dusk (unless there be a brighter planet, near ecliptic; check tables pages 134–135); **Capella** in Charioteer, yellowish, high northwest; **Arcturus** in Herdsman, orange, northeast; **Rigel** in Orion, bluish white, southwest, going down; **Procyon** in Little Dog, yellow-white, high west of south; **Betelgeuse** in Orion, reddish, southwest; **Aldebaran** in Bull, orange, west, going down; **Pollux** in Twins, yellowish, high west, almost overhead; **Spica** in Virgin, bluish, rising south of east; **Regulus** in Lion, bluish white, high southeast.   At lat. 50°: **Vega** in

OLLOWING DATES & HOURS

EC 1..............3–5 am
EC 16............2–4 am
AN 1............1–3 am
AN 16 .... midn–2 am
EB 1 ...... 11 pm–1 am
EB 15 .... 10 pm–midn

CALENDAR CHART 3

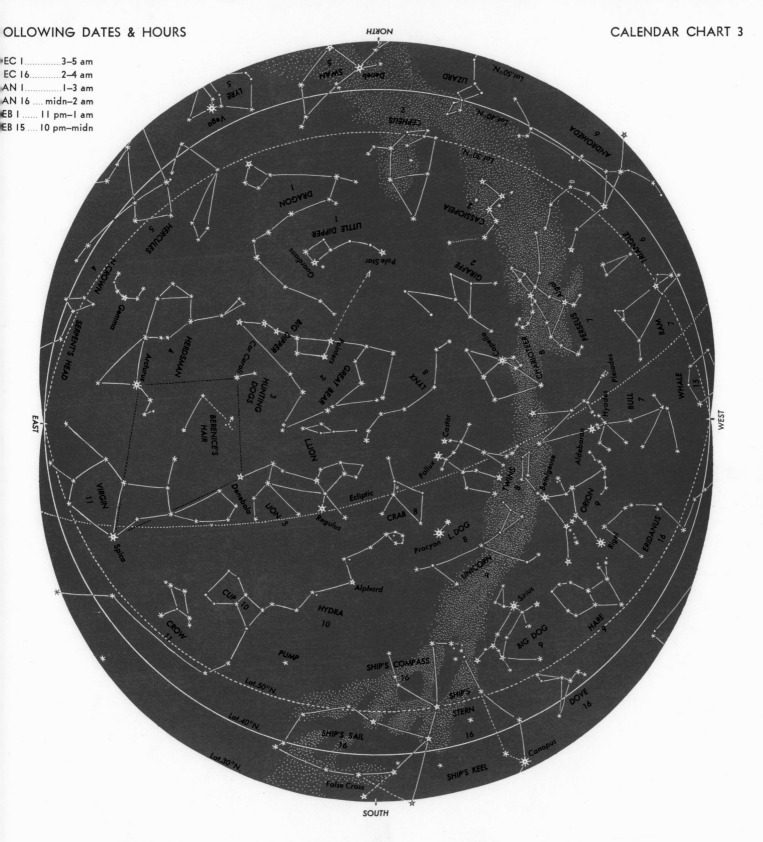

Lyre, bluish white, rising northeast, and **Deneb** in Swan, rising east of north. At lat. 30°: **Canopus** in Ship's Keel, yellowish-white, setting southwest. Arcturus and Spica, both on sweep of Dipper's handle, form with 3rd-mag. Cor Caroli and 2nd-mag. Denebola, in Lion's tail, the **Virgin's Diamond**, outlined on chart. Trace the Lion, high east of south: his shape is very lion-like; the peoples of the ancient Near East, to whom we owe this constellation, knew lions well. Look for Hydra's head high south and, above it, the Beehive in the Crab. If you are far south, look for the False Cross, due south; two hours later the true one, the famous Southern Cross, will come up from the southeast (chart 4). The Great Hexagon is now going; it won't return soon (chart 11).

MAGNITUDES

0  1  2  3  4  5

APR 1 ............9–11 p
APR 16 ..........8–10 p
MAY 1 .............dus
NOV 16 ............daw
DEC 1 ............5–7 an
DEC 16 ..........4–6 an

Ten 1st-mag. stars are visible at lat. 40°. In order of brightness: **Sirius** in Big Dog, bluish, setting southwest, much dimmed by ground air; **Vega** in Lyre, bluish white, rising northeast; **Capella** in Charioteer, northwest, going down; **Arcturus** in Herdsman, orange, halfway up east, first star you see at nightfall (except maybe planets, near ecliptic; check tables pages 134–135); **Procyon** in Little Dog, yellow-white, south of west, going down; **Betelgeuse** in Orion, reddish, low west; **Aldebaran** in Bull, orange, setting north of west; **Pollux** in Twins, yellowish, halfway down west; **Spica** in Virgin, bluish, southeast; **Regulus** in Lion, bluish white, high south. At lat. 50°: **Deneb** in Swan,

80

AN 1.............3–5 am
AN 16..........2–4 am
EB 1 .............1–3 am
EB 15 ..... midn–2 am
AR 1..... 11 pm–1 am
AR 16 ..10 pm–midn

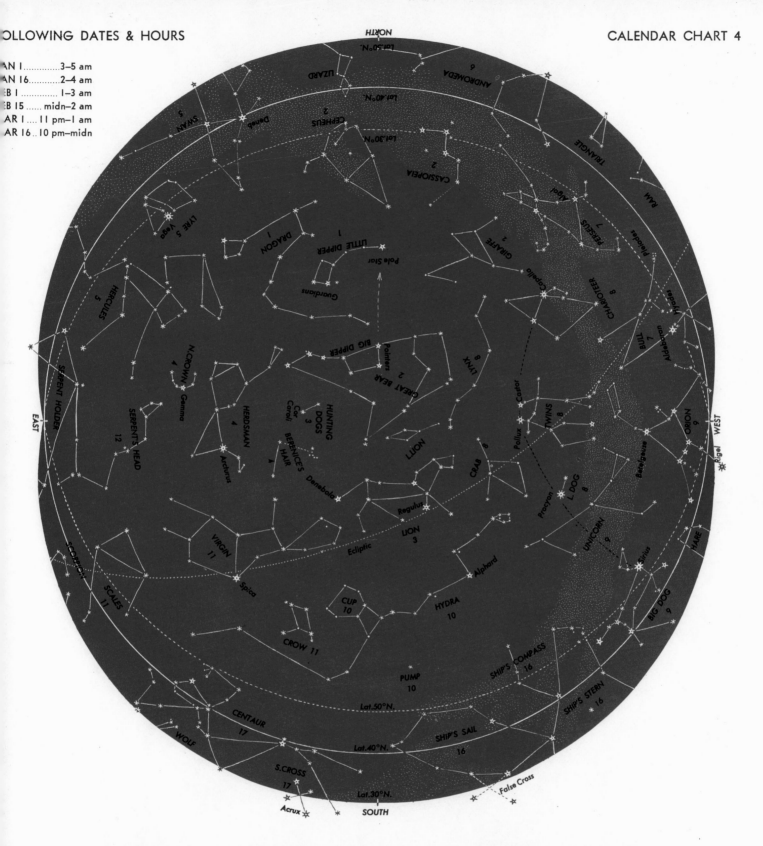

white, rising northeast. Twins, standing upright in west, Castor and Pollux forming the center of a vast crescent, with Procyon and Sirius to the left, and Capella and the bright star in the Charioteer's cap to the right. Southeast, look for the Virgin's Diamond (see preceding chart). Carnivores' Corner (see note page 34) is at its best: Great Bear, Lion, Little Lion, and Lynx almost overhead, and the Dragon rising; to trace the Great Bear, sit or lie down with feet pointing north. Don't search for the Milky Way: it is too close to the horizon to be seen well. If you are far enough south, about lat. 25° or more, you may see the Southern Cross rising low east of south, and the False Cross setting west of south.

MAY 1 .......... 9–11 p
MAY 16 ........ 8–10 p
JUNE 1 .............. du
DEC 16 ............ dav
JAN 1 .......... 5–7 a
JAN 16 .......... 4–6 a

MAGNITUDES

☀ ✷ ✩ ✦ ✱ ·
0  1  2  3  4  5

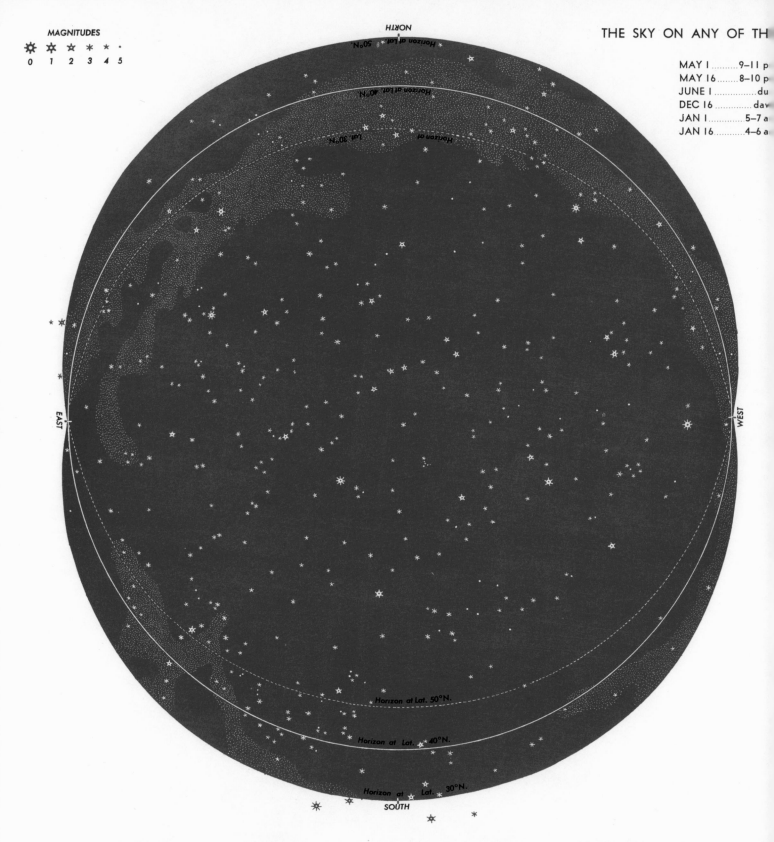

NORTH

Horizon at Lat. 50°N.

Horizon at Lat. 40°N.

Horizon at Lat. 30°N.

EAST

WEST

Horizon at Lat. 50°N.

Horizon at Lat. 40°N.

Horizon at Lat. 30°N.

SOUTH

Nine 1st-mag. stars are visible at lat. 40°.  In order of brightness: **Vega** in Lyre, bluish white, north-east, going up; **Capella** in Charioteer, yellowish, setting northwest; **Arcturus** in Herdsman, orange, almost overhead; barring planets (check tables pages 134–135), Arcturus is the first star you see at dusk since Vega and Capella, really a trifle brighter, are much lower in the sky and dimmed by ground air; **Procyon** in Little Dog, yellow-white, setting west; **Pollux** in Twins, yellowish, low north of west; **Spica** in Virgin, bluish, high south; **Antares** in Scorpion, reddish, rising southeast;

EB 1 .............. 3–5 am
EB 15 ............. 2–4 am
AR 1 ............. 1–3 am
AR 16 .... midn–2 am
PR 1 ...... 11 pm–1 am
PR 16 .... 10 pm–midn

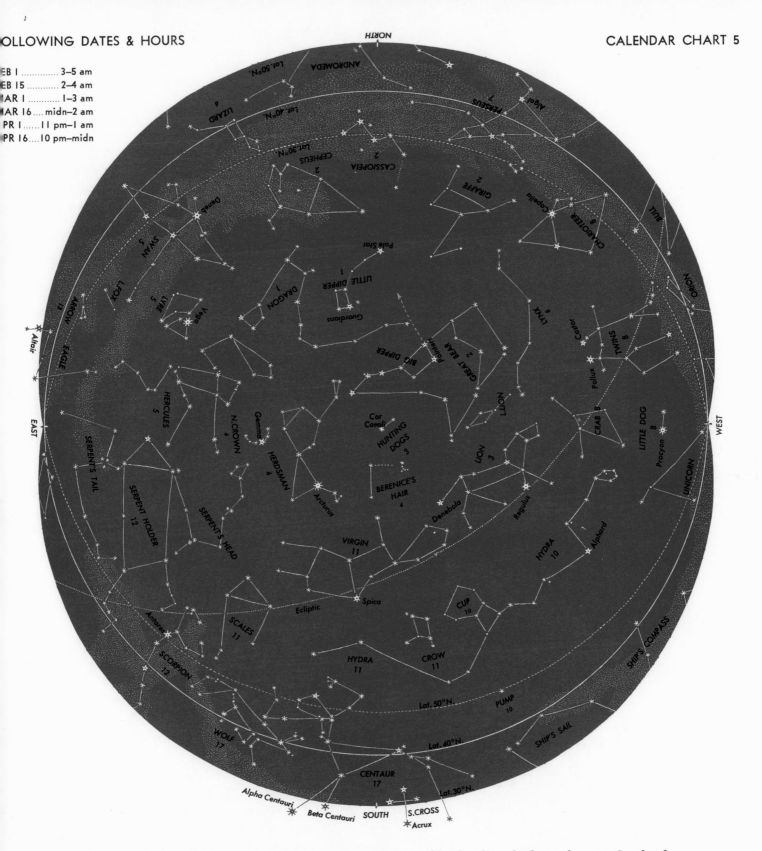

**Deneb** in Swan, white, rising northeast; **Regulus** in Lion, bluish white, high southwest.   South of lat. 30°: **Alpha** and **Beta Centauri,** in Centaur, rising, very low east of south, and **Acrux** in Cross, even lower, setting west of south.   Carnivores' Corner still high up (see preceding chart).   On clear dark nights sit or lie down to look for Berenice's Hair, overhead, a fuzz of faint stars.   No use looking for the Milky Way, it is too low to be seen.   Trace the Crow, below the Virgin, and if you are far enough south, lat. 25° or farther, look for the Southern Cross, just above the southern horizon, and try to trace Centaur and Wolf.

JUNE I ........ 9–11 p
JUNE 16 ...... 8–10 p
JULY I ............... du
JAN 15 ............ daw
FEB I ............ 5–7 a
FEB 15 ............ 4–6 a

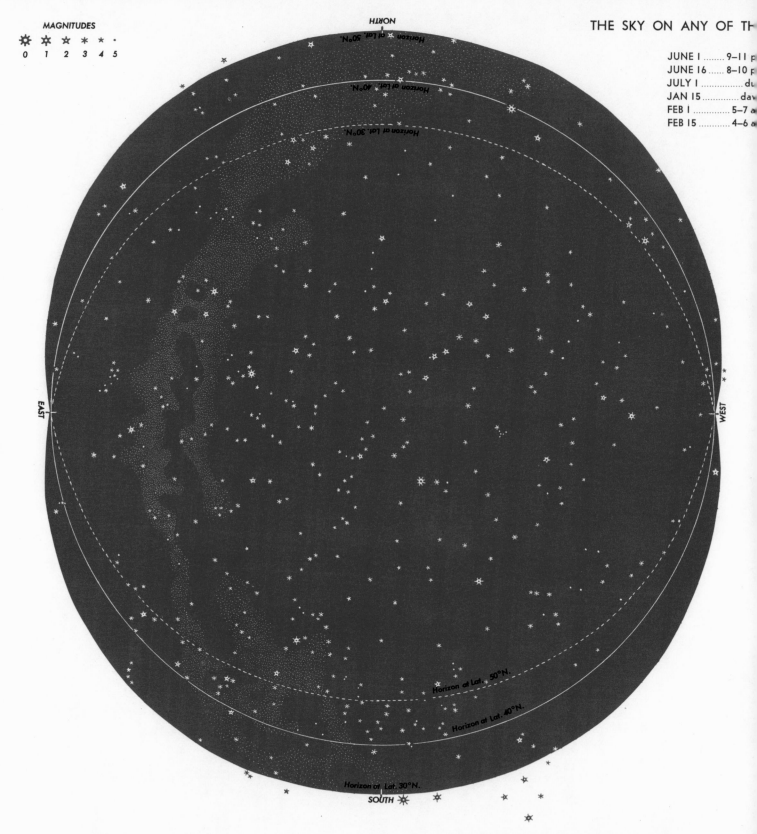

Eight 1st-mag. stars are visible at lat. 40°. In order of brightness: **Vega** in Lyre, bluish white, half-way up, east; **Arcturus** in Herdsman, orange, south, almost overhead; **Altair** in Eagle, yellow-white, east, going up; **Pollux** in Twins, yellowish, setting northwest; **Spica** in Virgin, bluish, west of south, going down; **Antares** in Scorpion, reddish, low east of south, going up; **Deneb** in Swan, white, north of east, going up; **Regulus** in Lion, bluish white, west, going down. At or near lat. 50° you still see **Capella,** low above northwest horizon. South of lat. 30° look for **Alpha** and **Beta Centauri,** west of

OLLOWING DATES & HOURS

MAR 1 ............ 3–5 am
MAR 16 ......... 2–4 am
PR 1 ............. 1–3 am
PR 16 ...... midn–2 am
MAY 1 .... 11 pm–1 am
MAY 16 .. 10 pm–midn

CALENDAR CHART 6

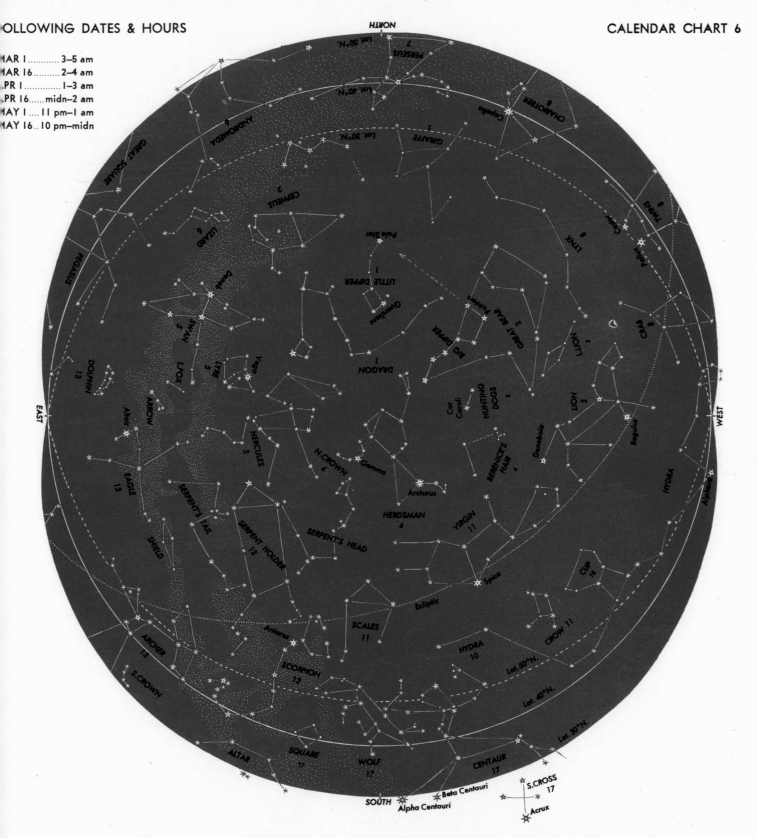

south, low above horizon. First stars you see at dusk (barring planets, see tables pages 134–135) are Arcturus and Vega, heralding summer. Good time for Hercules, standing upright, high east; look for star cluster in his keystone-shaped head. Near it is charming Northern Crown, easy to recognize. Look for "**Summer Triangle**," formed by Vega, Deneb, and Altair in Eagle's head, a row of three stars with Altair in the middle (see page 54). Watch Scorpion rise and don't miss Cat's Eyes in his tail. If you are far enough south you still see most of the Centaur. On clear, dark nights Milky Way is coming into view again, above eastern horizon.

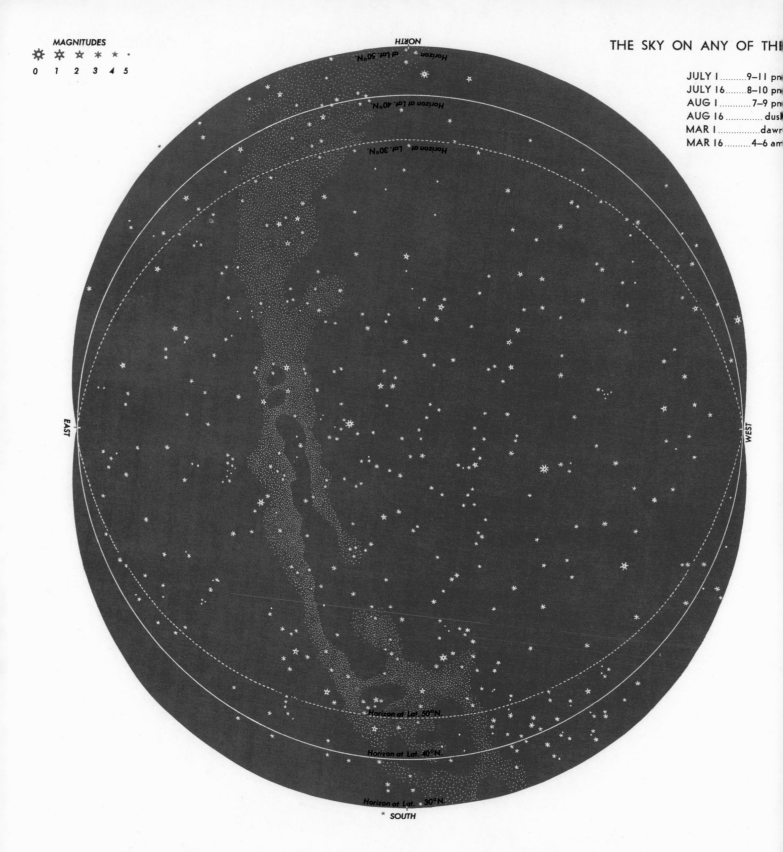

JULY 1 .......... 9–11 pm
JULY 16 ........ 8–10 pm
AUG 1 ............ 7–9 pm
AUG 16 ............. dusk
MAR 1 ............... dawn
MAR 16 ......... 4–6 am

Only six 1st-mag. stars are visible at lat. 40°.  In order of brightness: **Vega** in Lyre, bluish, almost overhead; **Arcturus** in Herdsman, orange, high southwest, going down; **Altair** in Eagle, yellow-white, high southeast, going up; **Spica** in Virgin, bluish, southwest, going down; **Antares** in Scorpion, reddish, south near its highest; **Deneb** in Swan, white, high up east.  If you are in the North Country you may see **Capella,** yellowish, very low north.  First star you see after dusk (except planets, see tables pages 134–135) is Vega, almost overhead.  Archer coming into good

FOLLOWING DATES & HOURS

CALENDAR CHART 7

APR 1 ............ 3–5 am
APR 16 ............ 2–4 am
MAY 1 ............ 1–3 am
MAY 16 .... midn–2 am
UNE 1 .... 11 pm–1 am
UNE 16 .. 10 pm–midn

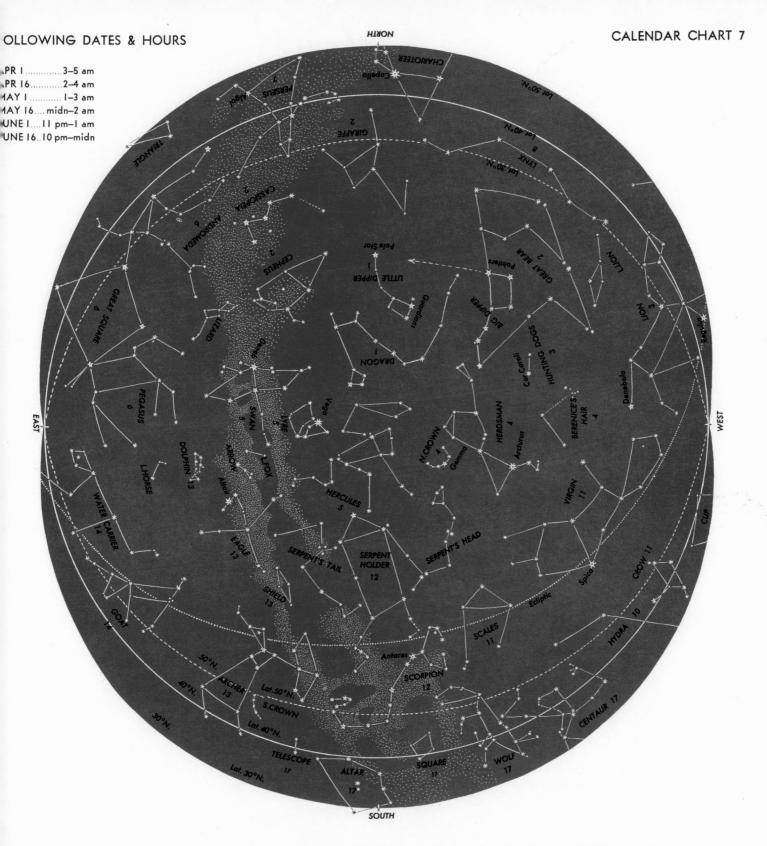

view above southeastern horizon. Look for Cat's Eyes in Scorpion's tail. Serpent Holder standing high above Scorpion in south, covering large region of sky; if you can trace the whole figure, serpent and all, you are good. Milky Way high in eastern half of the sky, with Swan almost overhead and Eagle a bit lower to the south; near Eagle's head (three stars in a row) look for Arrow and, just off Milky Way, Dolphin, small but charming, once seen not easily forgotten. Vega, Deneb, and Altair form "**Summer Triangle,**" a navigator's landmark.

AUG 1 ........... 9–11 pm
AUG 16 ........ 8–10 pm
SEPT 1 ........... 7–9 pm
SEPT 16 ......... 6–8 pm
OCT 1 ................... dusk
APR 16 ............... dawn

**MAGNITUDES**

0  1  2  3  4  5

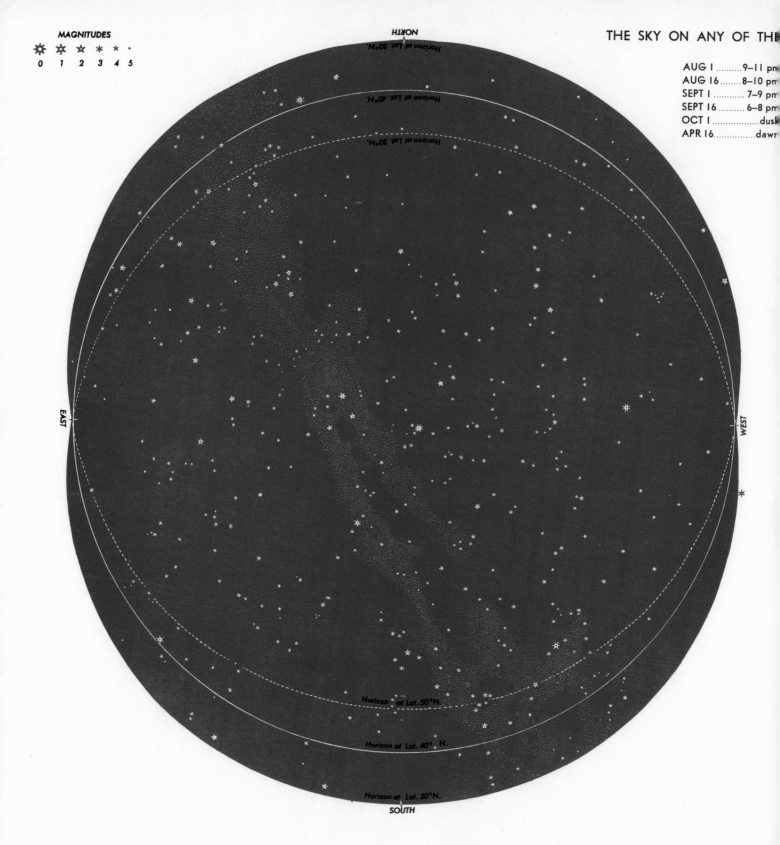

NORTH

Horizon of Lat. 50°N.

Horizon of Lat. 40°N.

Horizon of Lat. 30°N.

EAST

WEST

Horizon at Lat. 50°N.

Horizon at Lat. 40°. N.

Horizon at Lat. 30°N.

SOUTH

Only six 1st-mag. stars are visible at lat. 40°. In order of brightness: **Vega** in Lyre, bluish, overhead, first star you see at nightfall, barring planets; **Arcturus** in Herdsman, orange, west, going down; **Altair** in Eagle, yellow-white, high south; **Antares** in Scorpion, reddish, setting southwest; Fomalhaut in Southern Fish, white, rising southeast; **Deneb** in Swan, white, almost overhead. Watch horizon east of north to see **Capella** rise, by all means; the rise of a bright star is always worth watching, but you must know where to look. North of lat. 45° you'll miss Capella's rise, though; there she always remains above the horizon. Due south, Archer is at his best; skirt and feet may be hidden

88

MAY 1 .......... 3–5 am
MAY 16 ........ 2–4 am
JUNE 1 .......... 1–3 am
JUNE 16 .. midn–2 am
JULY 1 .... 11 pm–1 am
JULY 16 .. 10 pm–midn

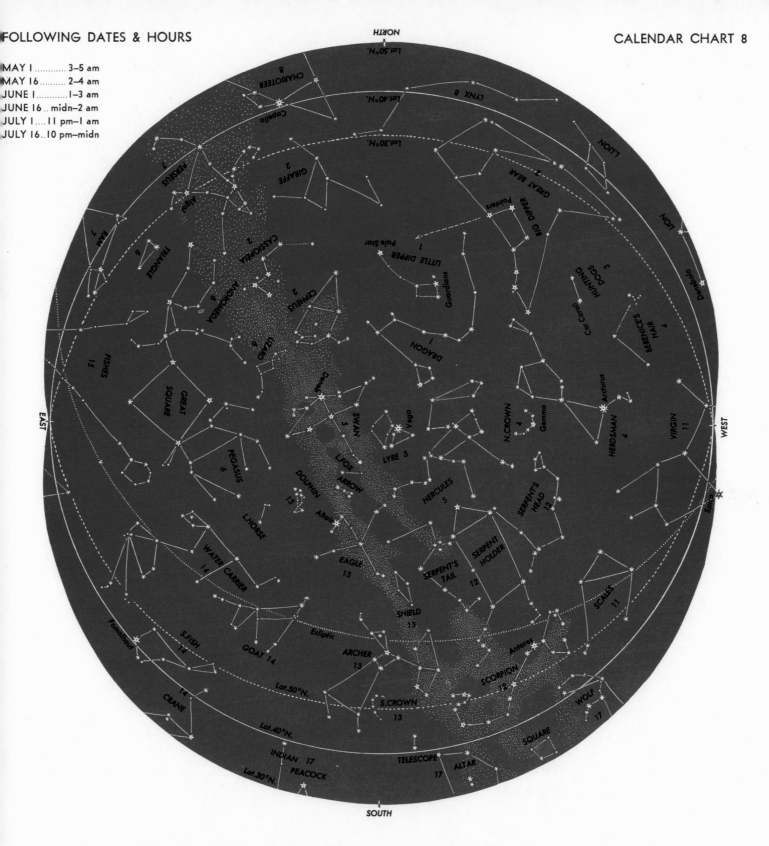

by ground haze, and so may Southern Crown, but both can be seen well if you are far enough south. Have a last look at the Scorpion, with the Cat's Eyes in his tail. As the Dipper moves down and Cassiopeia up, the Queen's suite begins to appear: Perseus, rising northeast, Andromeda, and Pegasus, with the Great Square above the eastern horizon. Under good conditions you can see the **Andromeda Nebula,** two million light-years away, the most distant object our unaided eye can see. The **Summer Triangle** (see preceding charts) is still overhead, but the rising in the southeast of the Goat, and the "wet" constellations Water Carrier, Fishes, and Southern Fish, foreshadows the coming of fall. Look for planets using tables pages 134–135.

SEPT 1 .......... 9–11 pm
SEPT 16 ........ 8–10 pm
OCT 1 .......... 7–9 pm
OCT 16 .......... 6–8 pm
NOV 1 .......... 5–7 pm
NOV 16 .............. dusk

MAGNITUDES

0 1 2 3 4 5

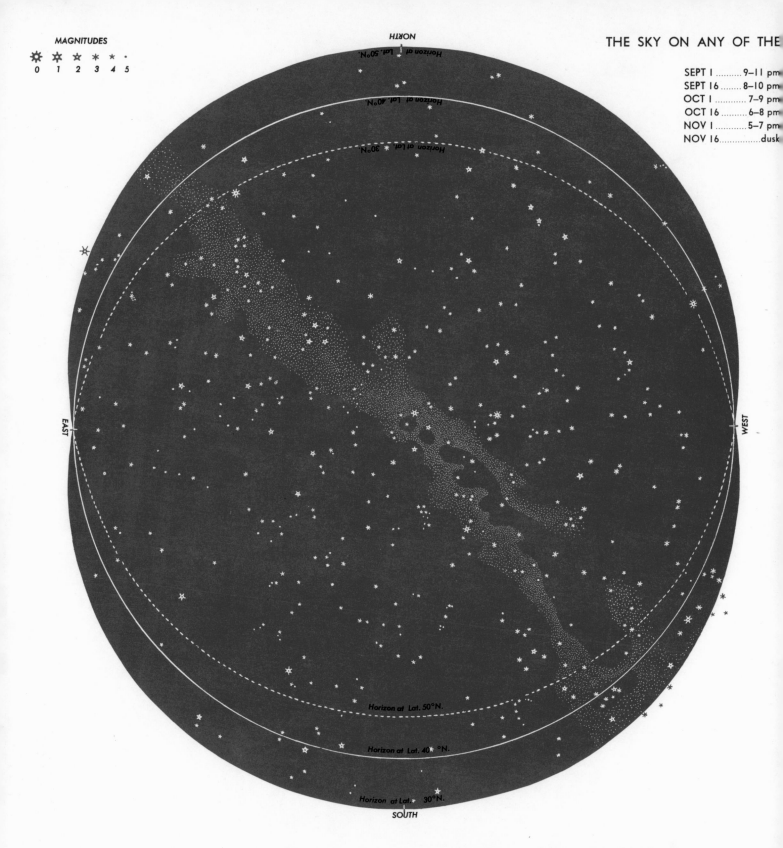

Horizon at Lat. 50°N.

Horizon at Lat. 40°N.

Horizon at Lat. 30°N.

NORTH

Horizon at Lat. 50°N.

Horizon at Lat. 40°N.

Horizon at Lat. 30°N.

EAST

WEST

SOUTH

Only six 1st-mag. stars are visible at lat. 40°. In order of brightness: **Vega** in Lyre, bluish white, west of zenith, first star you see at nightfall (except the brightest planets, see tables pages 134–135); **Capella** in Charioteer, yellowish, northeast, going up; **Arcturus** in Herdsman, orange, setting north of west; **Altair** in Eagle, yellow-white, high south; **Fomalhaut** in Southern Fish, white, east of south, going up; **Deneb** in Swan, near zenith. When you see Fomalhaut rise at nightfall autumn is there. A larger portion of the sky's "Wet Region" is now in view: Water Carrier (now at his highest), Southern Fish (with only Fomalhaut showing, the rest too dim to penetrate the ground haze),

UNE 1 ............. dawn
UNE 16 ......... 2–4 am
ULY 1 ........... 1–3 am
ULY 16 .... midn–2 am
AUG 1 .... 11 pm–1 am
AUG 16 .. 10 pm–midn

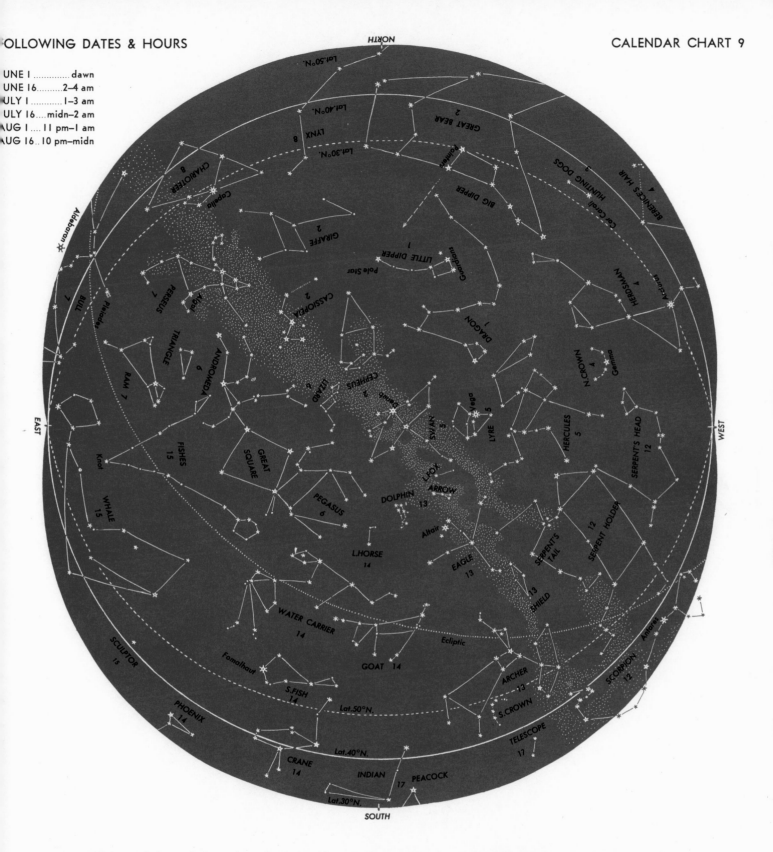

Fishes, and the Whale raising his snout, low in the southeast. Below Water Carrier, the Goat is at his highest, neither easy to trace nor very bright. If you are out early enough watch the **Pleiades** rise north of east, a charming sight, don't miss it, and an hour later Aldebaran and the Hyades. **Summer Triangle** still almost overhead, with Swan and Eagle winging toward each other in the brightest part of the Milky Way; worth lying down, with your feet pointing southwest, and looking straight up; the dark blotches in the Milky Way near Deneb are not holes but tremendous clouds of cosmic dust, *coal sacks* so called, hiding the stars behind them. When back on your feet look for the **Andromeda Nebula**.

91

OCT 1 ..........9–11
OCT 16 ........8–10
NOV 1 ...........7–9
NOV 16 ........6–8
DEC 1 ............5–7
DEC 16 ...............d

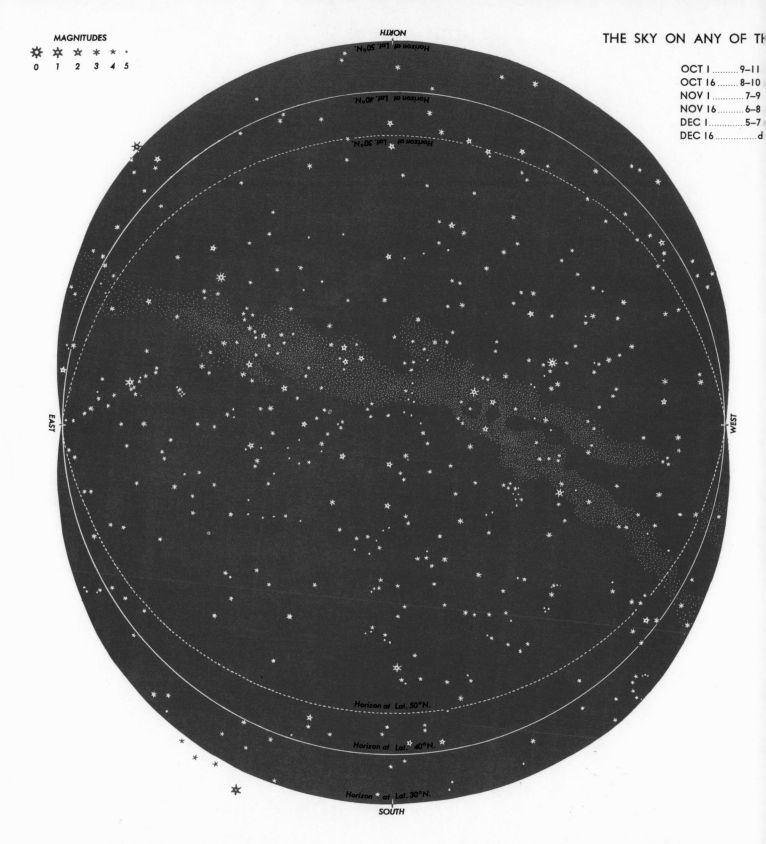

MAGNITUDES

0  1  2  3  4  5

NORTH

Horizon at Lat. 50°N.

Horizon at Lat. 40°N.

Horizon at Lat. 30°N.

EAST

WEST

Horizon at Lat. 50°N.

Horizon at Lat. 40°N.

Horizon at Lat. 30°N.

SOUTH

Only six 1st-mag. stars are visible at lat. 40°. In order of brightness: **Vega** in Lyre, bluish white, still high in west but going down, first star you see at nightfall (unless there is a brighter planet; see tables pages 134–135); **Capella** in Charioteer, yellowish, northeast, going up; **Altair** in Eagle, yellow-white, still high southwest but going down; **Aldebaran** in Bull, east, going up; **Fomalhaut** in Southern Fish, white, due south; **Deneb** in Swan, white, almost overhead going west. **Summer Triangle** (Vega–Deneb–Altair) still high in west but soon to go; autumn is marked by "Wet Region": Water Carrier, Southern Fish (with only Fomalhaut bright enough to be seen unless you

JULY 1 .............. dawn
JULY 16 .......... 2–4 am
AUG 1 ........... 1–3 am
AUG 16 .... midn–2 am
SEPT 1 .... 11 pm–1 am
SEPT 16 .. 10 pm–midn

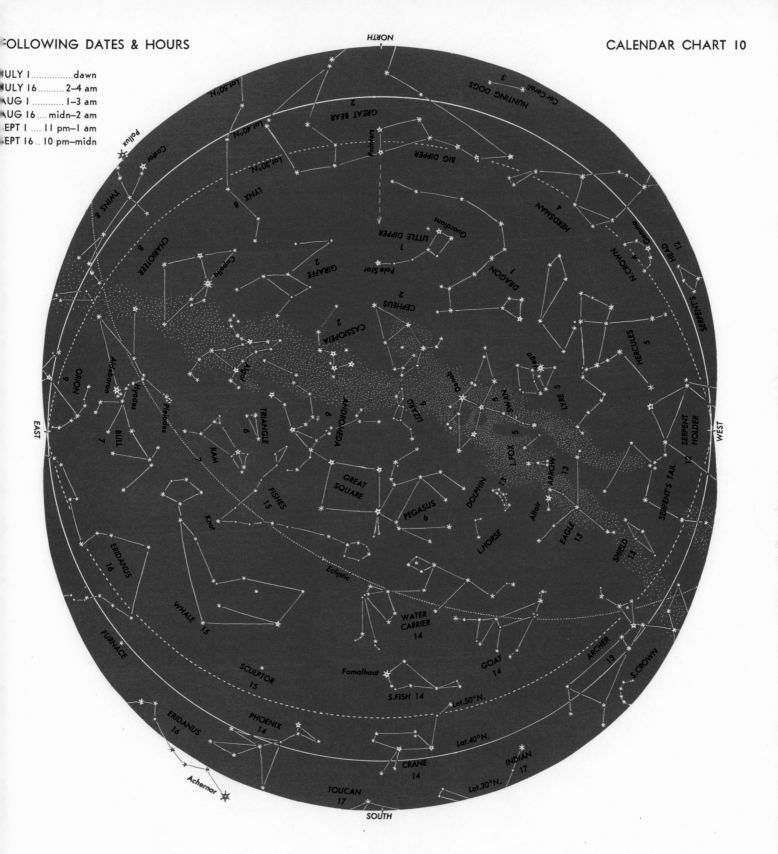

go far south), Fishes, Whale, and the River Eridanus. Pegasus, **Great Square,** and Andromeda near zenith; if the ground is not too cold, sit and look at our neighbor galaxy, the **Andromeda Nebula,** two million light-years away. A line from Polaris through first star in Cassiopeia's M, along eastern side of Great Square, and down through tip of Whale's snout, roughly marks the zero hour circle, the sky's Greenwich line, and a small v on the chart to the right of that imaginary line marks the spring equinox (see pages 114 and 119). Don't miss the **Pleiades** in the east, above Aldebaran.

NOV 1 .......... 9–11 pm
NOV 16 ....... 8–10 pm
DEC 1 ............. 7–9 pm
DEC 16 ......... 6–8 pm
JAN 1 ........... 5–7 pm
JAN 16 .............. dusk

MAGNITUDES

0 1 2 3 4 5

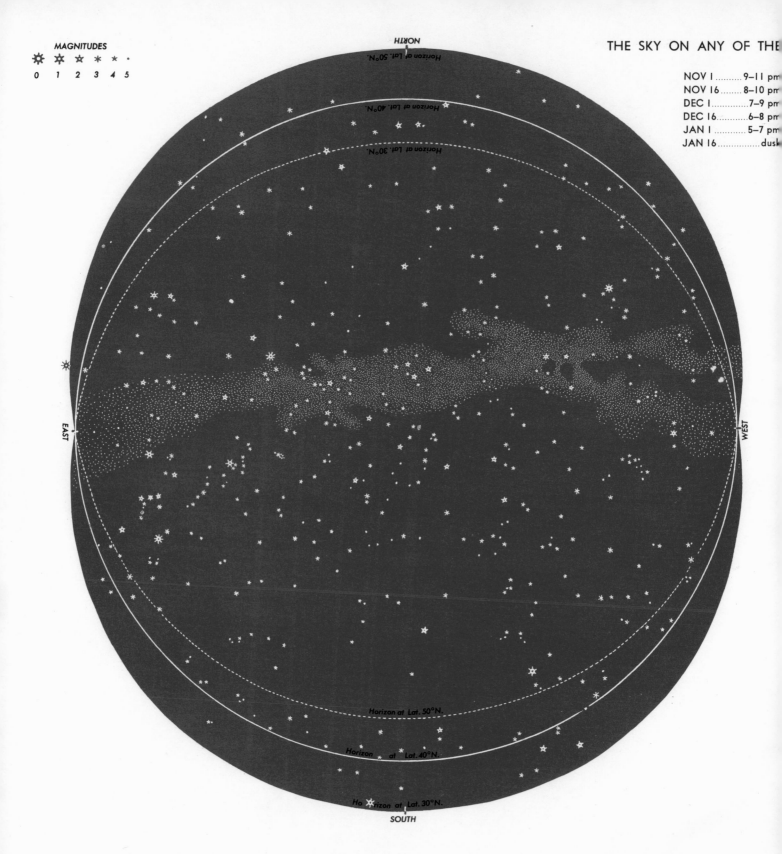

NORTH

Horizon at Lat. 50°N.

Horizon at Lat. 40°N.

Horizon at Lat. 30°N.

EAST

WEST

Horizon at Lat. 50°N.

Horizon at Lat. 40°N.

Horizon at Lat. 30°N.

SOUTH

Nine 1st-mag. stars are visible at lat. 40°. In order of brightness: **Vega** in Lyre, bluish white, northwest, going down, first star you see at nightfall (except maybe for planets, near ecliptic; see tables pages 134–135); **Capella** in Charioteer, yellowish, northeast, going up; **Rigel** in Orion, bluish white, rising south of east; **Altair** in Eagle, yellow-white, west, setting; **Betelgeuse** in Orion, reddish, rising east; **Aldebaran** in Bull, orange, above Betelgeuse; **Pollux** in Twins, yellowish, rising north of east; **Fomalhaut** in Southern Fish, white, setting southeast; **Deneb** in Swan, north of west, going down.— About lat. 30° bluish **Achernar**, in Eridanus, just rises above horizon in south. Constellations of "Wet Region," mostly dull, cover most of southern sky: Water Carrier, Southern Fish, Whale, Fishes,

94

OLLOWING DATES & HOURS

AUG 1 ............... dawn
AUG 16 .......... 2–4 am
EPT 1 ............ 1–3 am
EPT 16 .... midn–2 am
OCT 1 .... 11 pm–1 am
OCT 16 .. 10 pm–midn

CALENDAR CHART 11

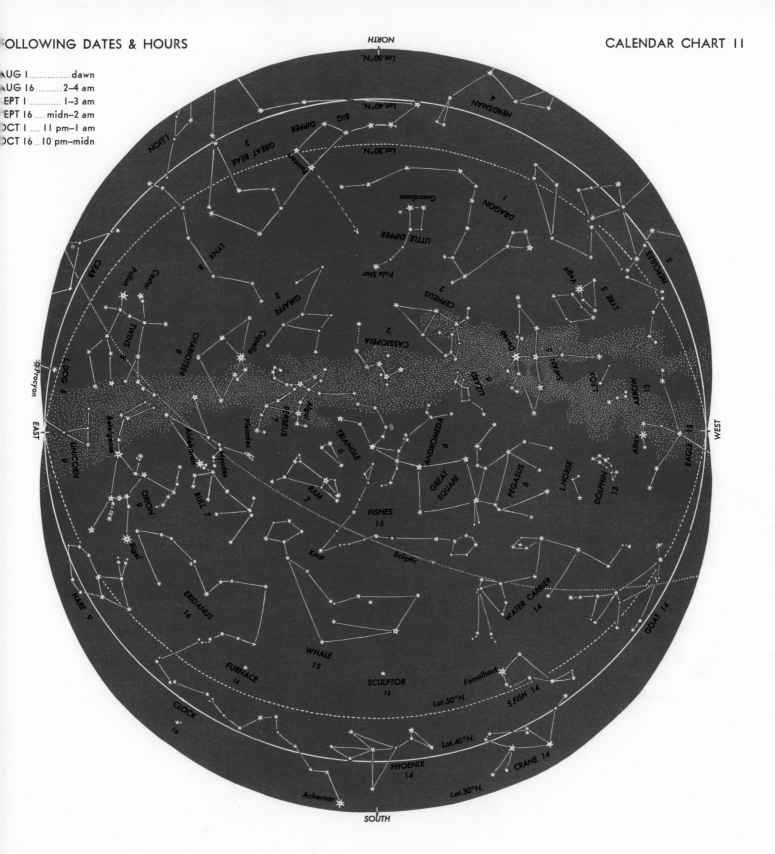

River Eridanus.  By contrast, many bright stars are lined up along Milky Way, running across the sky from east to west, and more are to come: watch horizon north of east for rising **Procyon** and, about 40 minutes later, for **Sirius,** brightest of all.  If you never tried Cepheus and Lizard, high in northwest, trace them now; it's not easy, though.  The **Summer Triangle,** souvenir of warmer nights, is setting fast.  Sit down on a chair and study Pegasus and Andromeda—the famous **Nebula** is now very near the zenith—and perhaps Ram and Fishes; the Western Fish, or Circlet, flounder-shaped, is easy to spot, south of the Great Square.  Don't miss the **Pleiades** high in the east.

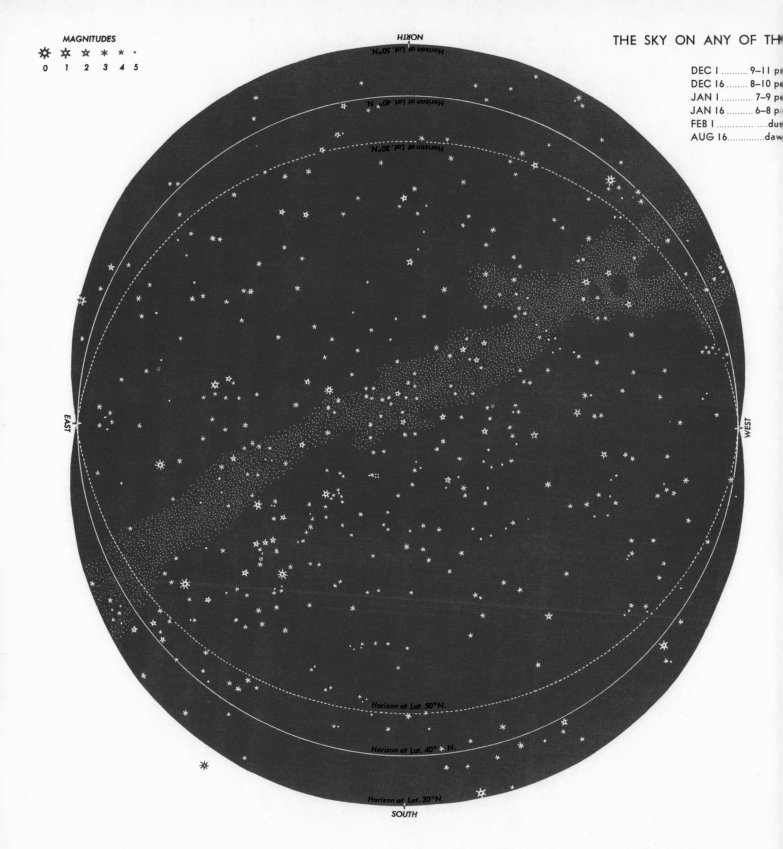

DEC 1 ......... 9–11 p
DEC 16 ....... 8–10 p
JAN 1 ........... 7–9 p
JAN 16 ........ 6–8 p
FEB 1 ................ dus
AUG 16 .......... daw

MAGNITUDES

0  1  2  3  4  5

NORTH

*Horizon at Lat. 50°N.*

*Horizon at Lat. 40°N.*

*Horizon at Lat. 30°N.*

EAST

WEST

*Horizon at Lat. 50°N.*

*Horizon at Lat. 40° N.*

*Horizon at Lat. 30°N.*

SOUTH

Nine 1st-mag. stars are visible at lat. 40°.  In order of brightness: **Sirius** in Big Dog, rising southeast, brightest of all stars, and first star you see at nightfall (except for planets, near ecliptic; check tables pages 134–135); **Vega** in Lyre, low northwest, setting; **Capella** in Charioteer, yellowish, almost overhead; **Rigel** in Orion, bluish white, southeast, going up; **Procyon** in Little Dog, yellow-white, south of east, going up; **Betelgeuse** in Orion, reddish, southeast, going up; **Aldebaran** in Bull, high southeast; **Pollux** in Twins, yellowish, north of east, going up; **Deneb** in Swan, white, northwest, going down.  At lat. 50°, **Regulus** in Lion is about to rise north of east.  At lat. 30°, **Achernar** in

FOLLOWING DATES & HOURS

SEPT 1 ............. 3–5 am
SEPT 16 ......... 2–4 am
OCT 1 ............. 1–3 am
OCT 16 .... midn–2 am
NOV 1 .... 11 pm–1 am
NOV 16 .. 10 pm–midn

CALENDAR CHART 12

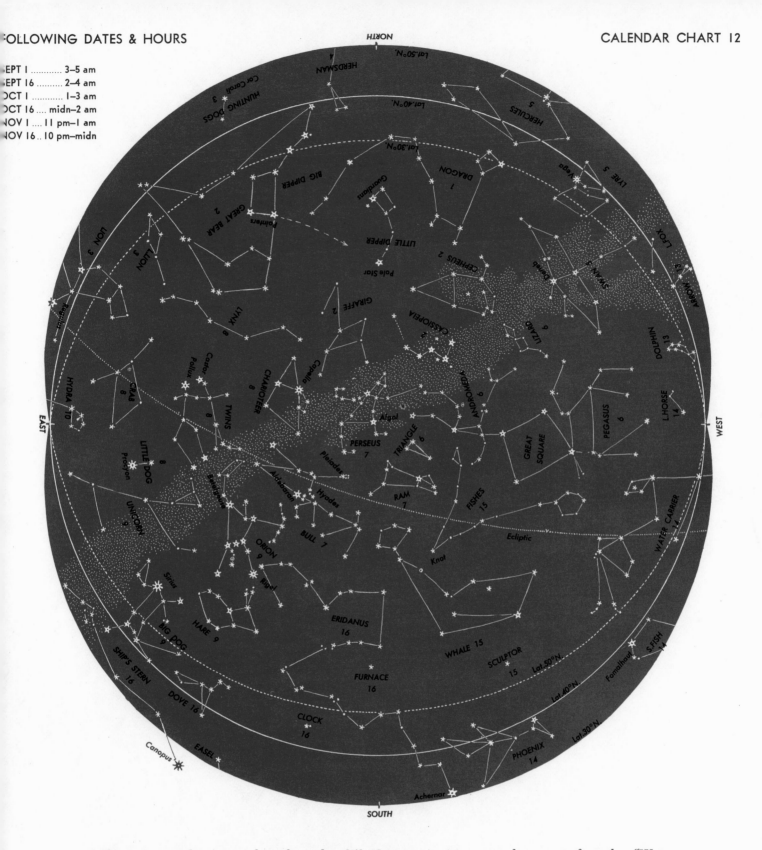

Eridanus is very low west of south; at lat. 25°, **Canopus** is rising, very low, east of south. "Wet Region," rather dull, fills most of southern sky; by contrast, eastern sky abounds with bright stars—seven of the twenty 1st-mag. stars form the **Great Hexagon,** marked on chart: Sirius, Procyon, Pollux, Capella, Aldebaran, Rigel at its corners, and Betelgeuse inside. · If you are in a sporting mood try to trace the large figure of the Whale, or all of the Bull, and if you have glasses use them on the **Pleiades,** and also on the **Hyades,** the V-shaped group to the right of Aldebaran, and on the **Andromeda Nebula,** almost overhead; sitting down will make it easier to look up and to hold the glasses steady. Watch eastern horizon for the rising of Regulus.

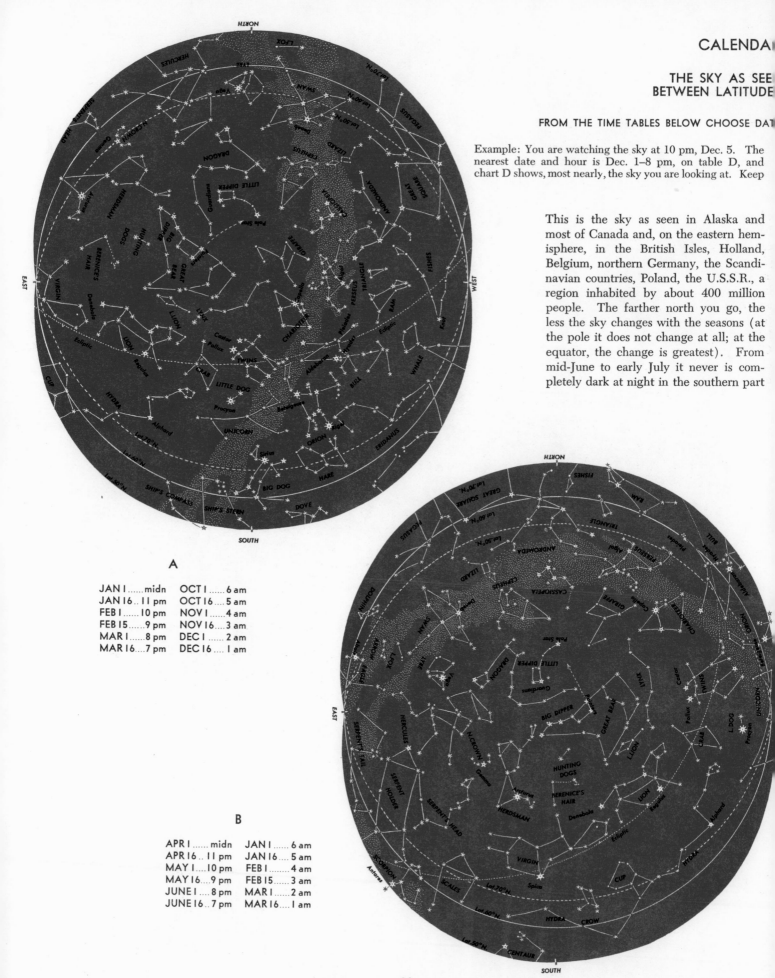

THE SKY AS SEE
BETWEEN LATITUDE

FROM THE TIME TABLES BELOW CHOOSE DAT

Example: You are watching the sky at 10 pm, Dec. 5. The nearest date and hour is Dec. 1–8 pm, on table D, and chart D shows, most nearly, the sky you are looking at. Keep

This is the sky as seen in Alaska and most of Canada and, on the eastern hemisphere, in the British Isles, Holland, Belgium, northern Germany, the Scandinavian countries, Poland, the U.S.S.R., a region inhabited by about 400 million people. The farther north you go, the less the sky changes with the seasons (at the pole it does not change at all; at the equator, the change is greatest). From mid-June to early July it never is completely dark at night in the southern part

A

| JAN 1......midn | OCT 1......6 am |
|---|---|
| JAN 16.. 11 pm | OCT 16....5 am |
| FEB 1......10 pm | NOV 1....4 am |
| FEB 15......9 pm | NOV 16....3 am |
| MAR 1......8 pm | DEC 1......2 am |
| MAR 16....7 pm | DEC 16....1 am |

B

| APR 1......midn | JAN 1......6 am |
|---|---|
| APR 16.. 11 pm | JAN 16....5 am |
| MAY 1....10 pm | FEB 1........4 am |
| MAY 16...9 pm | FEB 15......3 am |
| JUNE 1....8 pm | MAR 1......2 am |
| JUNE 16..7 pm | MAR 16....1 am |

CHART 13

ROM ANY PLACE
)° AND 70° NORTH

ND HOUR OF YOUR OBSERVING TIME

in mind, however, that by 10 pm the stars shown in the westernmost part of chart D will have set and some of the stars shown in the center part of chart A will have risen.

of this zone (in fact, anywhere north of lat. 48½°), hence only the brightest stars can be seen then; north of the arctic circle (lat. 66½°) you have midnight sun at that time. At the pole, as everybody knows, the sun never sets during spring and summer, but night lasts from early fall continuously till late winter. Up to lat. 55° north you can still use Calendar Charts 1–12; farther north use these charts alone or in combination with charts 1–12.

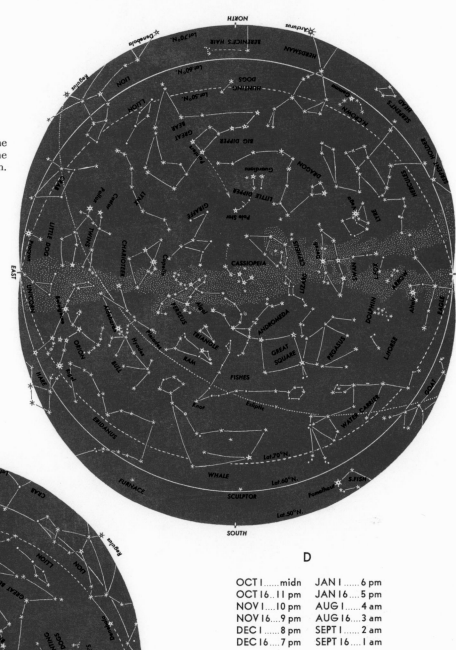

**D**

| | |
|---|---|
| OCT 1 ......midn | JAN 1 ...... 6 pm |
| OCT 16..11 pm | JAN 16....5 pm |
| NOV 1....10 pm | AUG 1......4 am |
| NOV 16....9 pm | AUG 16....3 am |
| DEC 1 ......8 pm | SEPT 1 ...... 2 am |
| DEC 16....7 pm | SEPT 16....1 am |

**C**

| | |
|---|---|
| JULY 1 .... midn | OCT 1 .....6 pm |
| JULY 16..11 pm | APR 16.....5 am |
| AUG 1....10 pm | MAY 1......4 am |
| AUG 16....9 pm | MAY 16...3 am |
| SEPT 1 ......8 pm | JUNE 1 .....2 am |
| SEPT 16....7 pm | JUNE 16.. 1 am |

99

MAGNITUDES

0   1   2   3   4   5

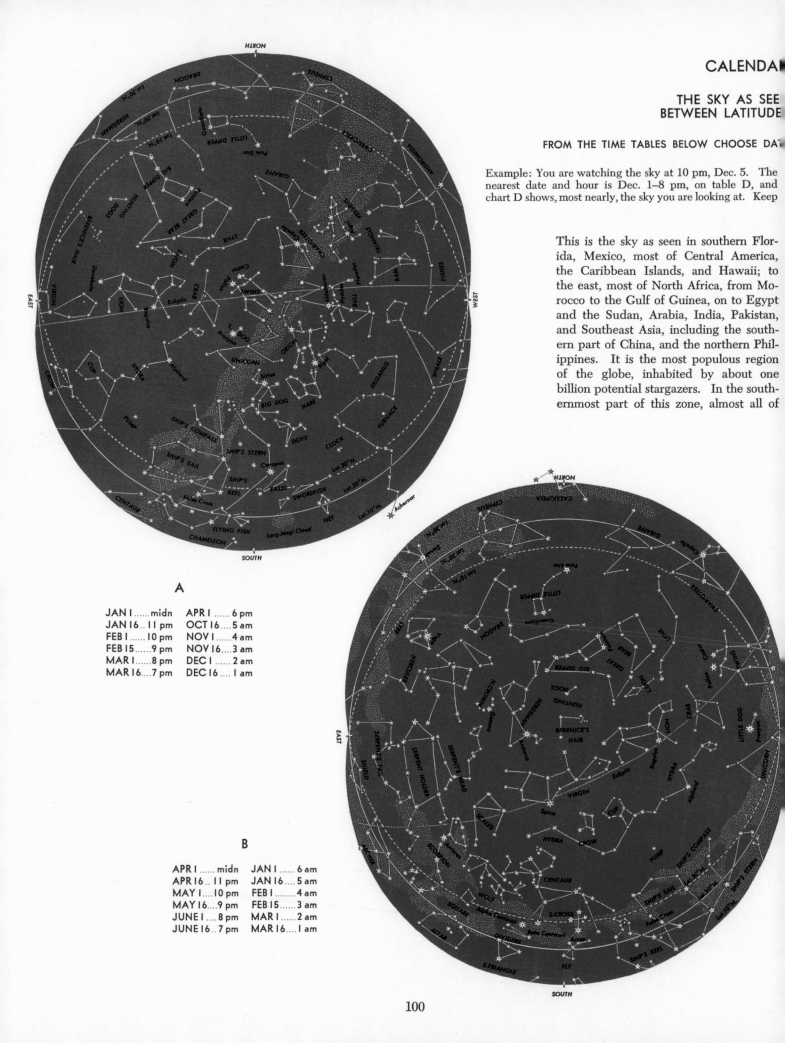

THE SKY AS SEE
BETWEEN LATITUDE

FROM THE TIME TABLES BELOW CHOOSE DA

Example: You are watching the sky at 10 pm, Dec. 5. The nearest date and hour is Dec. 1–8 pm, on table D, and chart D shows, most nearly, the sky you are looking at. Keep

This is the sky as seen in southern Florida, Mexico, most of Central America, the Caribbean Islands, and Hawaii; to the east, most of North Africa, from Morocco to the Gulf of Guinea, on to Egypt and the Sudan, Arabia, India, Pakistan, and Southeast Asia, including the southern part of China, and the northern Philippines. It is the most populous region of the globe, inhabited by about one billion potential stargazers. In the southernmost part of this zone, almost all of

**A**

| | |
|---|---|
| JAN 1......midn | APR 1......6 pm |
| JAN 16..11 pm | OCT 16....5 am |
| FEB 1....10 pm | NOV 1.....4 am |
| FEB 15.....9 pm | NOV 16...3 am |
| MAR 1.....8 pm | DEC 1......2 am |
| MAR 16....7 pm | DEC 16....1 am |

**B**

| | |
|---|---|
| APR 1......midn | JAN 1......6 am |
| APR 16..11 pm | JAN 16....5 am |
| MAY 1....10 pm | FEB 1........4 am |
| MAY 16...9 pm | FEB 15......3 am |
| JUNE 1....8 pm | MAR 1......2 am |
| JUNE 16..7 pm | MAR 16....1 am |

CHART 14

FROM ANY PLACE
0° AND 10° NORTH

AND HOUR OF YOUR OBSERVING TIME

mind, however, that by 10 pm the stars shown in the
esternmost part of chart D will have set and some of the
ars shown in the center part of chart A will have risen.

the southernmost constellations come into
view, at one time or another, low above
the southern horizon. In latitudes of the
upper twenties use this chart in combination with charts 1–12 which show all
1st-mag. stars and cover most of the
U.S., part of Canada, the countries of
Europe south of lat. 55°N, from Portu-
gal to the Caspian Sea, the Middle East,
and on to north China and Japan, with
a total population of more than 800
million.

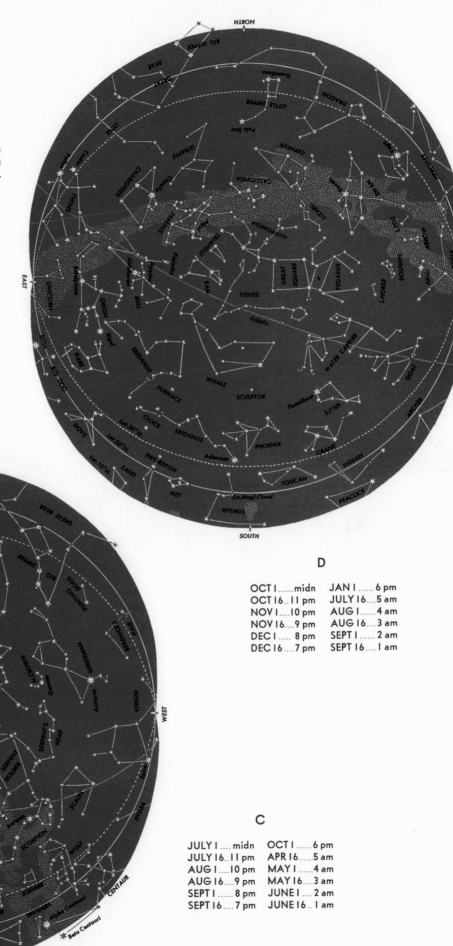

**D**

| | |
|---|---|
| OCT 1......midn | JAN 1......6 pm |
| OCT 16..11 pm | JULY 16....5 am |
| NOV 1....10 pm | AUG 1......4 am |
| NOV 16....9 pm | AUG 16....3 am |
| DEC 1..... 8 pm | SEPT 1......2 am |
| DEC 16....7 pm | SEPT 16....1 am |

**C**

| | |
|---|---|
| JULY 1....midn | OCT 1......6 pm |
| JULY 16..11 pm | APR 16.....5 am |
| AUG 1....10 pm | MAY 1......4 am |
| AUG 16....9 pm | MAY 16....3 am |
| SEPT 1......8 pm | JUNE 1....2 am |
| SEPT 16....7 pm | JUNE 16..1 am |

MAGNITUDES

0  1  2  3  4  5

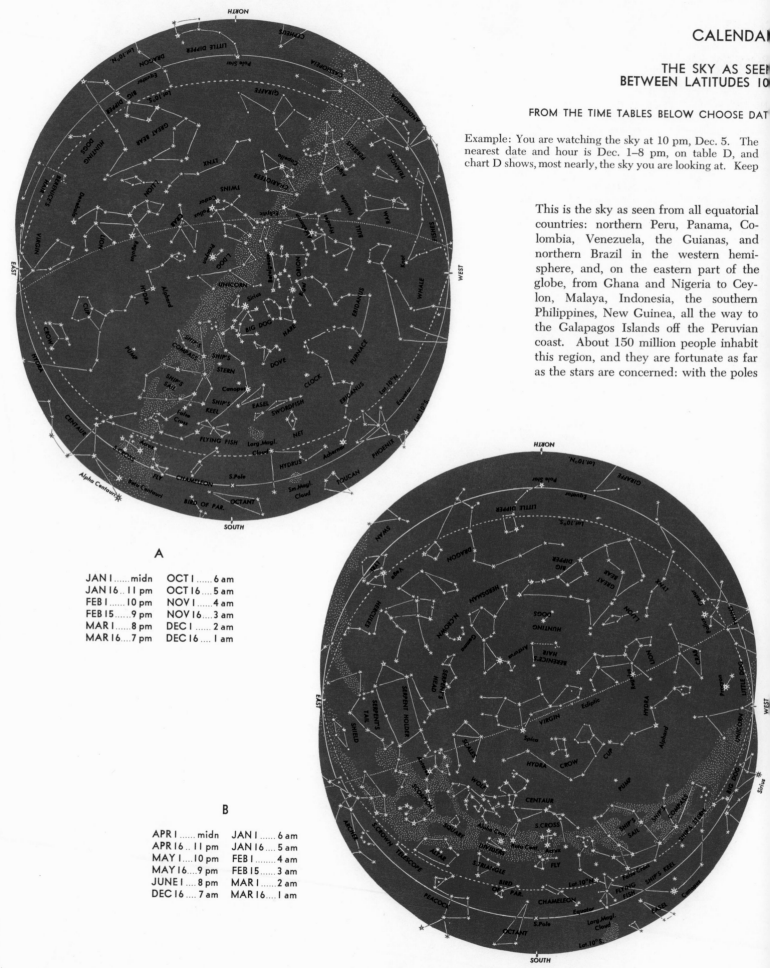

THE SKY AS SEEN
BETWEEN LATITUDES 10

FROM THE TIME TABLES BELOW CHOOSE DAT

Example: You are watching the sky at 10 pm, Dec. 5. The nearest date and hour is Dec. 1–8 pm, on table D, and chart D shows, most nearly, the sky you are looking at. Keep

This is the sky as seen from all equatorial countries: northern Peru, Panama, Colombia, Venezuela, the Guianas, and northern Brazil in the western hemisphere, and, on the eastern part of the globe, from Ghana and Nigeria to Ceylon, Malaya, Indonesia, the southern Philippines, New Guinea, all the way to the Galapagos Islands off the Peruvian coast. About 150 million people inhabit this region, and they are fortunate as far as the stars are concerned: with the poles

**A**

| | |
|---|---|
| JAN 1......midn | OCT 1......6 am |
| JAN 16..11 pm | OCT 16....5 am |
| FEB 1......10 pm | NOV 1......4 am |
| FEB 15.....9 pm | NOV 16...3 am |
| MAR 1......8 pm | DEC 1......2 am |
| MAR 16....7 pm | DEC 16....1 am |

**B**

| | |
|---|---|
| APR 1......midn | JAN 1......6 am |
| APR 16..11 pm | JAN 16....5 am |
| MAY 1....10 pm | FEB 1......4 am |
| MAY 16...9 pm | FEB 15......3 am |
| JUNE 1....8 pm | MAR 1......2 am |
| DEC 16....7 am | MAR 16....1 am |

CHART 15

ROM ANY PLACE
NORTH AND 10° SOUTH

ND HOUR OF YOUR OBSERVING TIME

in mind, however, that by 10 pm the stars shown in the westernmost part of chart D will have set and some of the stars shown in the center part of chart A will have risen.

on or near the horizon, all the constellations can be seen here (see figure 18, page 117) at one time or another; the length of night varies little (about 40 minutes at lat. 10° north or south and practically not at all on the equator), and no midnight sun will ever interfere with their observations. Note that south of the equator the seasons are inverted: spring begins on or about September 23, followed by summer on or about December 21, and so on.

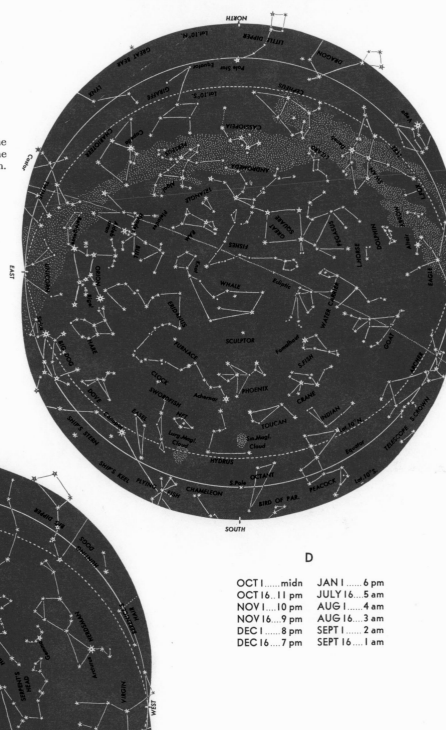

**D**

| OCT 1......midn | JAN 1......6 pm |
|---|---|
| OCT 16..11 pm | JULY 16....5 am |
| NOV 1....10 pm | AUG 1......4 am |
| NOV 16....9 pm | AUG 16....3 am |
| DEC 1......8 pm | SEPT 1......2 am |
| DEC 16....7 pm | SEPT 16....1 am |

**C**

| JULY 1....midn | OCT 1......6 pm |
|---|---|
| JULY 16..11 pm | APR 16.....5 am |
| AUG 1....10 pm | MAY 1......4 am |
| AUG 16....9 pm | MAY 16....3 am |
| SEPT 1......8 pm | JUNE 1....2 am |
| SEPT 16....7 pm | JUNE 16..1 am |

MAGNITUDES

☆ ☆ ☆ ★ ✴ ·
0   1   2   3   4   5

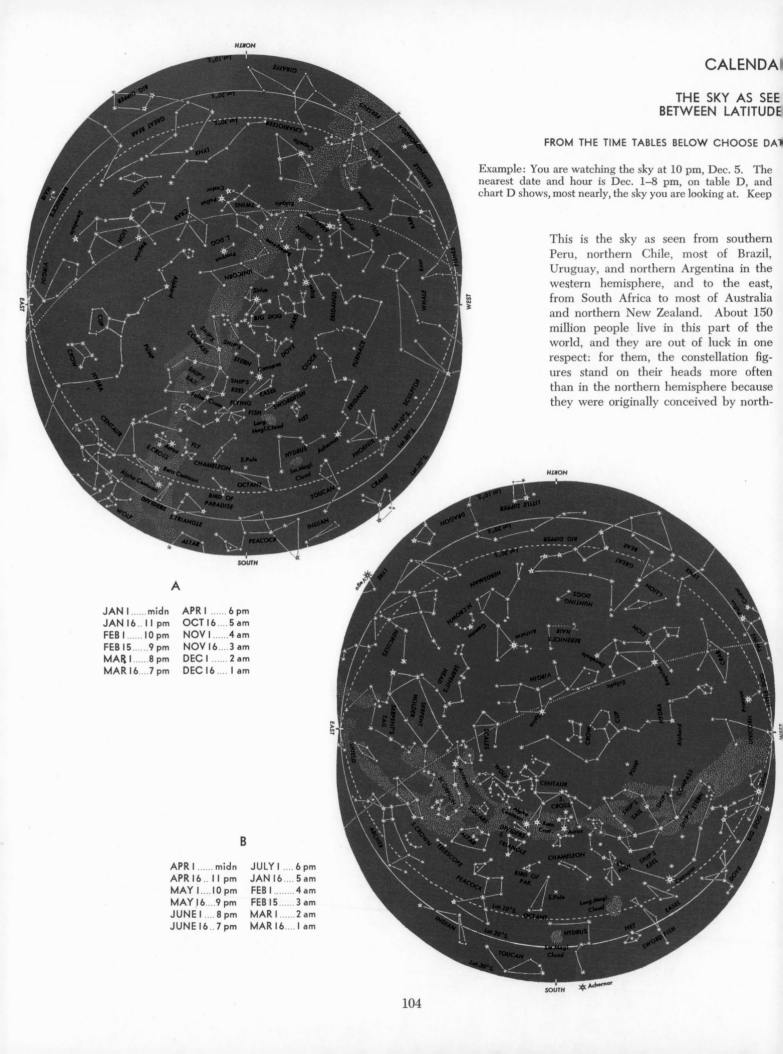

Example: You are watching the sky at 10 pm, Dec. 5. The nearest date and hour is Dec. 1–8 pm, on table D, and chart D shows, most nearly, the sky you are looking at. Keep

This is the sky as seen from southern Peru, northern Chile, most of Brazil, Uruguay, and northern Argentina in the western hemisphere, and to the east, from South Africa to most of Australia and northern New Zealand. About 150 million people live in this part of the world, and they are out of luck in one respect: for them, the constellation figures stand on their heads more often than in the northern hemisphere because they were originally conceived by north-

**A**

| JAN 1......midn | APR 1 ...... 6 pm |
|---|---|
| JAN 16..11 pm | OCT 16....5 am |
| FEB 1......10 pm | NOV 1......4 am |
| FEB 15......9 pm | NOV 16....3 am |
| MAR 1......8 pm | DEC 1 ...... 2 am |
| MAR 16....7 pm | DEC 16 .... 1 am |

**B**

| APR 1 ...... midn | JULY 1 ....6 pm |
|---|---|
| APR 16..11 pm | JAN 16....5 am |
| MAY 1....10 pm | FEB 1........4 am |
| MAY 16....9 pm | FEB 15......3 am |
| JUNE 1....8 pm | MAR 1......2 am |
| JUNE 16..7 pm | MAR 16....1 am |

# CHART 16

## FROM ANY PLACE
## 10° AND 30° SOUTH

### AND HOUR OF YOUR OBSERVING TIME

in mind, however, that by 10 pm the stars shown in the westernmost part of chart D will have set and some of the stars shown in the center part of chart A will have risen.

ern observers who could not know that, one day, there might be stargazers "down under." As on all other charts, the brighter stars that are a little below the horizon are shown on the white of the page so that, with a little practice, these charts can be used as far south as southern New Zealand and the southern tip of South America; south of those regions, no permanent human habitations exist, so there is not much need for a further set of charts.

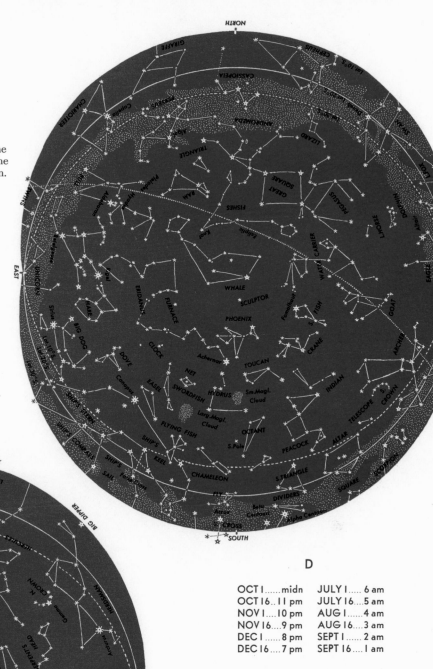

**D**

| | |
|---|---|
| OCT 1......midn | JULY 1......6 am |
| OCT 16...11 pm | JULY 16....5 pm |
| NOV 1....10 pm | AUG 1......4 am |
| NOV 16....9 pm | AUG 16....3 am |
| DEC 1......8 pm | SEPT 1......2 am |
| DEC 16....7 pm | SEPT 16....1 am |

**C**

| | |
|---|---|
| JULY 1....midn | OCT 1......6 pm |
| JULY 16..11 pm | APR 16......5 am |
| AUG 1....10 pm | MAY 1......4 am |
| AUG 16....9 pm | MAY 16....3 am |
| SEPT 1......8 pm | JUNE 1......2 am |
| SEPT 16....7 pm | JUNE 16..1 am |

**MAGNITUDES**

0 1 2 3 4 5

PART 4

# SOME WHYS AND HOWS

*...and I am telling you the earth is a globe, not a disc!*

So FAR we have limited ourselves to the constellations and their shapes, to some of the stars that compose them, and where to spot them in the sky at different times of the night, through the year.

If we have made this material our own, or the better part of it, we are well at home among the stars, which was our chief aim. We could now converse on more than equal terms with that ancient Chaldean shepherd we conjured up at the beginning (provided we spoke his tongue) and, if we cared to, impress most of our contemporaries with our superior knowledge of the heavens.

Many will want to stop here, and they can do so without harm. No matter what part of nature one studies—microbes or Milky Ways—there is a point where one begins but never an end. It's more than a lifetime job, and most of us have other things to mind, sometimes to our regret.

But some want to go a bit further. The subject is fascinating, and a number of questions have come up which were hardly answered, and terms had to be used which could stand more explaining.

The following chapters contain such answers and explanations, but within the limits of this field book we can take up only a few important points and treat them only briefly. On the other hand, repetitions cannot always be avoided—a forgivable sin, if committed only where the context requires it.

Those who wish to extend their studies beyond the range of this book will have no trouble obtaining ample and reliable material. They will find a few suggestions in the list of books on page 160.

We shall keep things as untechnical as possible (it's the long way; technical formulations are short cuts), but we cannot do entirely without angles, degrees, great circles, planes, and the like. This by way of a last warning, and here we go!

**BUILDING A SKY MODEL:** If we want to get beyond the "Chaldean stage" in our comprehension of the stars, we must obtain a smattering of what is known as celestial mechanics. This includes the *apparent* motion of the sky as a whole as well as the *real* motion of the earth around itself and around the sun, which produces this apparent motion; and elements such as meridian, celestial equator, declination, hour circle, ecliptic, sidereal time must be explained.

This could be done in one single diagram containing all those elements. That would be easier for the author but make it hard for many a reader. We shall therefore proceed in stages, from the very simple toward the complex, by constructing, on these pages, a model of the sky: a planetarium more realistic than the umbrella on page 22, which was no more than a stopgap.

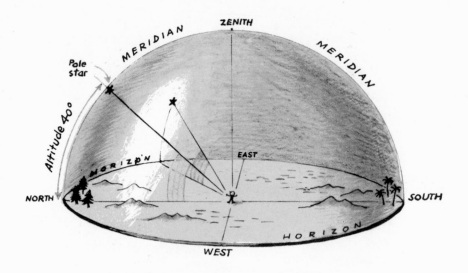

Figure 10:   The Sky We See: A Half Globe

We shall start simply with what we see.   We see the earth—if our view is unobstructed—as a flat, circular disc.   The border of this disc is the horizon.   We are in the exact center of it (no matter where we go, we are always in the center of "our" horizon).   Over us we see the sky, a vast hollow half-globe, the rim of which sits on the horizon.

Figure 10 is a model of this setup.   In the center of the disc is a Lilliputian observer.   Throughout this project, imagine yourself in his shoes and visualize what he sees.   Suppose our model represents the sky as seen from a place 40° latitude north, then the observer sees the Pole Star about[1] 40° above the horizon, due north.   The distance of a star from the horizon is called its ALTITUDE. The Pole Star, therefore, has an altitude of about 40°.   The altitude of the other star on this figure is about 25°.   As a star wanders across the sky—or appears to be wandering—its altitude changes. The Pole Star's altitude however remains nearly the same unless the observer moves to a different *latitude*.   The Pole Star's or, more exactly, the celestial pole's altitude always equals the observer's latitude.   We shall find out *why* on page 116.

The (imaginary) line which the observer can draw from the north point on the horizon, through pole and zenith and down on the other half of the sky dome (the southern half) to the south point on the horizon, is the MERIDIAN, an important line, as we shall see.

A line from observer to celestial pole marks the axis around which we must make the model sky turn so that the observer sees his sky rotate, from east to west.

We realize at once that a *half-globe* will not do.   If we set it turning around the axis, a gap would appear on the east side, and part of the half-globe would slide below the horizon on the west side.

We overcome this difficulty if, instead of a half-globe, we use a *full globe*.   The observer inside sees only the globe's upper half, of course.   The other half is underneath the ground he is standing on, below the horizon.   We now prolong the axis underneath the disc; it pierces the disc in the

[1] If the Pole Star were *exactly* on the north celestial pole, its altitude at latitude 40° would be *exactly* 40°. The Pole Star is about 1° off the true pole but we may neglect this small difference in the present demonstration.

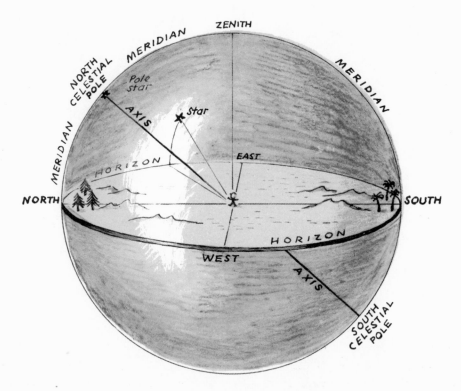

Figure 11: The Sky as a Full Globe

center, where the observer is, and meets the lower half of the globe at a point exactly opposite the north celestial pole: the *south celestial pole*. While the globe turns around this axis, the position of the disc in the globe remains unchanged: it does not move, only the surrounding sky does, as the observer sees it.

If stars are attached to the globe, and the globe rotates, what does the Lilliputian observer see from the center of our miniature planetarium?

To keep things simple we will consider just one star, the one we saw on the previous picture, about 25° above the northeastern horizon. On the next figure we shall have a look at the course which the observer sees the star describe as the globe rotates.

NOTE: It took mankind a long time to conceive the sky as a full globe. The Greeks seem to have had this idea first. Our friend from Chaldea—whom we are now leaving far behind—thought that the stars, and also the sun, moon, and planets, moved across the vaulted sky overhead, from east to west, and then crawled back along the flat underside of the earth disc, to rise again over the eastern rim of the disc, in due course.

On the other hand, we must keep in mind that the sky globe is not a *real* globe in the sense that the earth is. Strictly speaking there is no such thing as a sky, only stars on a background of void. Yet the sky globe is neither an arbitrary assumption nor an optical illusion. We actually see one half of the hollow globe at any moment, with the other half unseen but coming into sight as the sphere appears to rotate. The sky globe has no size expressible in miles or square miles. We can call its diameter infinite or indefinite if we like; it does not matter much; we don't use the diameter as a measuring unit as we do on solid spheres. Instead, distances on the sky are measured in degrees (from horizon to zenith is 90°, once around the horizon 360°)—and surfaces, in square degrees.

111

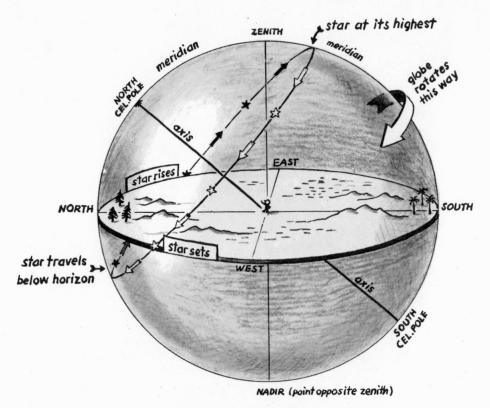

Figure 12: The Sky Globe Rotates

As the globe slowly rotates from E to W, the observer inside sees the star move upward at an angle. At its highest point it is exactly on the *meridian,* and after crossing the meridian it descends slowly on the western half of the sky. It goes down with the same slant as when it rose, only in the opposite sense, and sets below the western horizon. For a while, as the globe goes on turning, the star travels below the horizon and the observer cannot see it until it rises above the eastern horizon.

The points of rising and setting are equally far away from the horizon's north point. If a star rises, say, due NE, it sets due NW; if it rises SE by E, it sets SW by W, and so on, and any star (but not sun, moon, and planets) always rises and sets at the same points (seen from the same locality) throughout the year, only at different times.

All stars, and also sun, moon, and planets, are at their highest—they *culminate*—when they cross the meridian. When the sun crosses the meridian, we have *noon* (*meridian* from Latin *meridies,* noon). The average time span from one noon to the next is a day[1]—the ordinary day we all live by. But to the astronomer this is not just a day but a SOLAR or SUN DAY (from Latin *sol,* sun). He also has the SIDEREAL or STAR DAY (from Latin *sidus,* star): the time span, very nearly,[2] between two successive culminations of a star. From one culmination to the next the star makes a full turn—apparently. In reality the earth does the turning, and the sidereal day is therefore, very nearly, the period of the true rotation of the earth in relation to the stars.

The sidereal day is about four minutes shorter (the four minutes mentioned on page 66) than the solar day, and its subdivisions: sidereal hours, minutes, seconds, are proportionally shorter than solar hours, minutes, seconds. We shall see the reason for this difference on page 122.

---

[1] We count our days from midnight to midnight, though. Otherwise we should have to change dates every noon, and lunch might begin on Tuesday and end on Wednesday.

[2] Very nearly because the sidereal day is measured not by the culminations of a *star* but by two successive culminations of the *vernal equinox* (see figure 19) which is not stationary but moving slowly. The difference is very small—0.008 second a day, or one day in 25,800 years—and results from the "wobble" of the earth's axis, described on page 128.

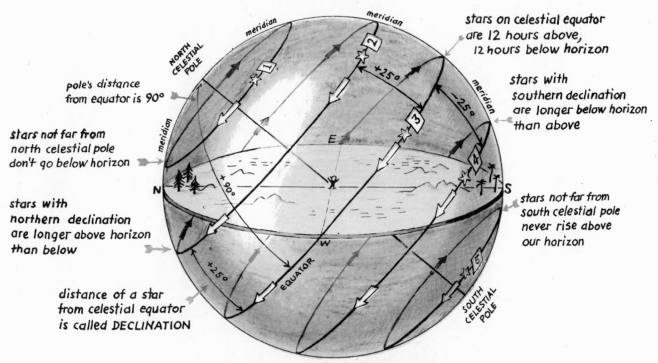

Figure 13: Parallels of Declination

We now attach a few more stars to the rotating globe: star 1 not far from the north celestial pole; star 2 somewhat farther away; star 3 halfway between north and south poles; star 4 closer to south pole than to north pole; and star 5 not far from the south pole.

The observer inside the globe sees *star 1* circle around the north pole without ever going below the horizon. *Star 2* goes below the horizon for a while but is longer above the horizon than it is below. *Star 3*, halfway between the two poles, is half the time above the horizon, half the time below. Since one rotation takes 24 (sidereal) hours, this star is visible 12 hours. It rises due east and sets due west. *Star 4*, rising about southeast and setting southwest, spends more time below the horizon than above; and *star 5*, close to the south celestial pole, does not rise above the horizon at all; the observer never sees it.

The lines which mark the paths of the five stars are parallel. They look very much like circles of latitude, or parallels, on a terrestrial globe. In fact the celestial globe has such (imaginary) parallel circles; they are called PARALLELS OF DECLINATION. The particular circle which divides the celestial globe in two, into a northern and a southern celestial hemisphere, is called the CELESTIAL EQUATOR. Its declination is 0° (just as the earth's equator is latitude 0°), and the declination of each star is measured from there, in degrees. *Star 2* on the figure, for instance, has a declination of 25° north (written: Dec.+25°), while *star 4* has a declination of 25° south (written: Dec.—25°).

Since the celestial equator—and with it all the parallels of declination—always keeps its distance from the celestial poles, its place in the sky, for an observer, does not change unless the observer moves to a different latitude.

You can visualize the celestial equator any night if you can remember a few star groups which are on it or near it: Orion's Belt; Hydra's head; the Virgin; the Eagle's left wing tip; Water Carrier's head; the Whale's tail.

While the *altitude* of a star changes during the night, as the star rises or sets, its *declination* (distance from the celestial equator) *does not*. It tells where on the celestial sphere the star is to be found, at any time, but does not tell all. If we say a star has a declination of 25° north, it could be anywhere on the circle, 25° north of the celestial equator. Just as on the terrestrial globe, we must give the star's longitude. How this is done, we will see on the next pages.

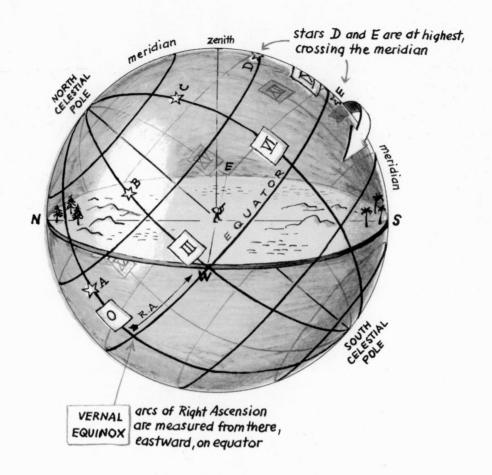

Figure 14:   Hour Circles

What are circles of longitude on the terrestrial globe, are called *hour circles* on the celestial globe.  The hour circle of a star is one half of a great circle going from north to south celestial pole, passing through the star.  On our model the half-circle marked O is the hour circle of star A; star B is on the hour circle marked III; star C is on the VI hour circle, and D and E are on the IX hour circle.

There are 24 hour circles, from O to XXIII, and they are counted eastward on the celestial equator from a point in the *Fishes* called the VERNAL, or SPRING, EQUINOX (see page 119, figure 19). The hour circle going through this point is the ZERO HOUR CIRCLE.  Each hour circle, being only one half of a great circle, has a counterpart which complements it to a full circle.  To the zero hour circle this is the XII hour circle; to I hour circle, XIII hour circle; and so on: you can see it dimly on the sketch.[1]

As the sky rotates the hour circles rotate too.  When an hour circle is at its highest it coincides with the meridian.  At that moment all stars on that hour circle culminate.  Stars on the same hour circle culminate at the same time (on the sketch, stars D and E are culminating) but, having different declinations, they do not rise and set at the same time.  When the zero hour circle is on the meridian the *sidereal day* begins: it is O h sidereal time, a moment as important to the astronomer as midnight or noon is to the ordinary citizen.  One (sidereal) hour after the O h circle has passed the meridian, I h circle passes it—at 1 h sidereal time; after another hour, at 2 h

[1] The hour circles are marked on the UNIVERSAL SKY CHART on pages 158–59 as well as on the star chart inside the jacket of this book.

114

sidereal time, II h circle passes the meridian, and so on. After twenty-four sidereal hours, O h circle passes the meridian again and a new sidereal day begins.

Hour circle and parallel of declination define the place of a star on the celestial globe, as longitude and latitude define a place on earth. But instead of writing "hour circle" the astronomer usually gives the RIGHT ASCENSION (R.A. for short) of a star. This is the arc, on the equator, measured eastward from the vernal equinox to the point where the star's hour line crosses the equator. It is expressed in hours, minutes, and seconds. A star on Hour Line XIX has R.A. 19. The full "address" of a star—say CAPELLA—reads: R.A. 5$^h$13$^m$ Dec.+45°57′ ("Dec.+" = North Declination). This not only tells you the star's place among its companions, but also that it culminates at 5$^h$13$^m$ sidereal time every day and that, being halfway between pole and equator, it is visible most of the time in our latitudes.

On the foregoing pages, we referred to the fact that the pole's altitude equals the observer's latitude; that the hour circles are measured from the vernal equinox (which is one of the two points where the ecliptic—the sun's apparent path—crosses the celestial equator); and that the sidereal day is about four minutes shorter than the solar day, but we did not explain those facts nor describe the elements involved.

We shall do this now, and in connection therewith have a look at the zodiac; at the causes for our seasons; and at the shift of the celestial poles through the ages caused by the "wobble" of the earth's axis.

In addition, let us briefly consider planets and moon, as well as the galaxy of which our solar system is an infinitesimal part. We shall conclude with a quick glance at the history of the constellations and at the possibilities of life outside our earth.

stars appear circling counterclockwise

☆ *Polaris*

line of vision
from earth's pole
to celestial pole
coincides with
earth's axis

lines of vision
from latitude 40°

line of vision
from earth's
equator

LAT. 40°

EQUATOR

## POLE STAR AND LATITUDE

Ours is an age of travel. Thousand-mile trips are trivial affairs, and many a stargazer has an opportunity to watch the skies change as he journeys north or south for any great distance. The shape of the constellations remains of course unaffected but he finds that, say, in southern Florida Polaris stands quite low, about 25° above the horizon, and he sees some constellations he did not see when a few days ago he looked at the stars from northern Minnesota, where he saw the Pole Star more than half way up toward the zenith.

To put it precisely (as stated on page 110): the altitude of the celestial pole equals the observer's latitude. The altitude changes as the observer moves north or south, and the *axis around which he sees the whole star sphere turn appears less or more tilted according to his higher or lower latitude.* This fact permits him to determine his latitude by watching the stars. It is an important fact, but so far we have not explained it. So here is why.

On figure 15 we have the earth with an observer standing at the earth's north pole and looking at Polaris through a telescope. The Pole Star, true, is not exactly on the celestial pole but we can neglect the small difference for a moment. Since the celestial pole is the point to which the earth's axis points, he must look up vertically to see the Pole Star. As the earth under him turns from west to east, the stars around Polaris are circling around the pole, so it seems to him, counterclockwise; Polaris itself remains in its place, or nearly.

But if he moves away from the earth's north pole, Polaris is no longer overhead. The farther south he goes the farther down must he tilt his telescope to look at it, and if he moves to the earth's southern hemisphere Polaris will sink below his horizon.

That much we see from the picture.[1] We also see that, as long as the observer remains on the same parallel—say, the 40th—the tilt of his telescope remains the same as he looks at Polaris, and this goes for all circles of latitude, including the equator.

[1] The sinking of the Pole Star as the observer moves southward is hard to visualize for some, although it is easy to comprehend in geometrical terms. This may help you: tilt the page slowly so that the little man, first on lat. 40°, then on the equator, comes to stand upright, and watch Polaris all the while: you can actually see it sink lower and lower from its overhead position, as you tilt.

Figure 15:  Pole Star and Latitude

But we cannot see from figure 15 what exactly the tilt has to be, on a given latitude, because on the scale of this drawing with a one-inch earth, Polaris would have to be many miles away instead of a few inches, and all lines of vision, from any point of this small earth, to the celestial pole would be practically parallel (as they are in reality) instead of slightly converging, as on that drawing.

We therefore need a new drawing (figure 15A) where all lines of vision from different latitudes are parallel to the earth's axis which, as we know, coincides with the line of vision from the terrestrial to the celestial pole (axis of the celestial sphere). Now the Pole Star's or, more accurately, the celestial pole's altitude is the angle between the observer's line of vision to the celestial pole and the plane of the horizon, from any given point. If all lines of vision, from anywhere, are parallel, all we have to find out is: at what angle do they meet the plane of the horizon at given latitudes, keeping in mind that the plane of the horizon at any point on earth is perpendicular to the earth's radius at that point. (We may consider the earth as a perfect sphere in this demonstration and disregard its slight flattening at the poles.)

The latitude of a point being the angle between earth's radius and plane of equator, and its complement being equal to the altitude's complement (50° in our case) because both are on parallels, the two angles, latitude and altitude (colored blue on the sketch), are also equal; which is what we set out to show.

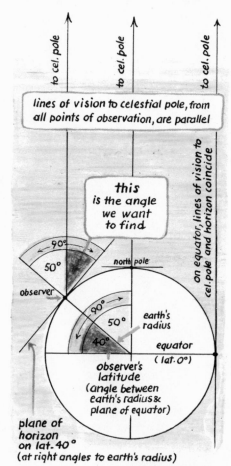

Figure 15A:   The Pole's Altitude

*Here are three examples illustrating the tilt of the sky sphere at different latitudes:*

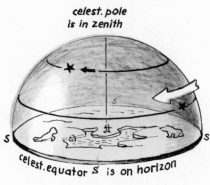

Figure 16

The Sky at the North Pole

Only northern half of celestial sphere visible at any time. Stars circle around pole parallel to horizon, don't rise or set. There is no east or west; all directions are south. Stars south of celestial equator permanently out of sight.

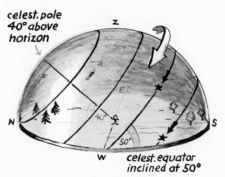

Figure 17

The Sky at 40° Latitude North

Axis of celestial sphere tilted at 40°. Stars north of celestial equator longer above horizon than below. Many, but not all, stars of south celestial hemisphere visible but below horizon longer than above. Celestial equator inclined 50° (R-40°) against plane of horizon.

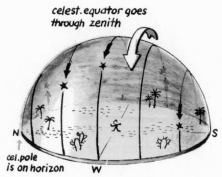

Figure 18

The Sky at the Equator

Axis of celestial sphere lies on plane of horizon. Pole Star on horizon (nearly). Exactly half of either celestial hemisphere—northern and southern —visible at all times, with celestial equator passing through zenith. Stars rise and set vertically, and all stars in entire sky can be seen at one time or another.

# ECLIPTIC AND SEASONS

The figure on the opposite page shows the earth and its ORBIT (its yearly course around the sun) inside a large hollow globe representing the celestial sphere. Marked on the sphere are the Pole Star, the axis of the celestial sphere, the celestial equator, and the zero hour circle which we discussed on page 114. Around the sphere, at an angle to the equator, runs a belt, here drawn in lighter color, with 12 constellations marked on it. This belt is the ZODIAC (we shall consider it on page 130), and along its middle runs a broken line, the ECLIPTIC—the apparent path of the sun among the stars in the course of a year.

A closer look at the drawing shows how this apparent path comes about:

The earth on its yearly course is shown in 4 positions: December 22, March 21, June 21, and September 23. As you study the model you can see how to an observer on the earth the sun would appear against a different background of stars as the earth proceeds along its orbit while the sky with its stars remains unmoved. (No misunderstanding: on this model we are not considering the *apparent daily motion of the sky* seen from an earth at rest, but the *real yearly motion of the earth* against a sky at rest.)

Now suppose an observer on the earth were in a balloon in the upper stratosphere where sun and stars are visible at the same time; he would see the sun against the *Archer* as background in December; against the *Fishes* in March; it would appear in the *Twins* in June, and in the *Virgin* in September; the following December it would be in the *Archer* again, and so on.[1]

If he plotted the sun's position among the stars from day to day on a star globe of his own, he would see it drift eastward by almost 1° daily (360° in 365¼ days) and after a year he would have plotted a great circle line around his globe, the same as on our drawing: the *ecliptic,* so called because eclipses of sun and moon occur along that line.

Now the earth not only revolves around the sun, it also turns around itself all the time, causing day and night. For reasons unknown even to the experts, it so happens that the *axis around which the planet turns does not stand perpendicular to the plane of the orbit,* but deviates from the vertical by 23½°.

If this were not so, if the axis stood vertical, day and night would be equal everywhere throughout the year, and there would be no seasons. Besides, figure 19 would look simpler and we would have nothing more to explain here. But since there *is* such a tilt, we do have a change of seasons and of the day's length, and an explanation is called for. So here it is:

The earth's axis being thus tilted, and the celestial axis being but the prolongation of the earth's axis, the celestial axis is tilted by the same angle, 23½°. The celestial equator, in turn, being perpendicular to the celestial axis, is inclined against the ecliptic by 23½° also, as figure 19 shows. The two great circles, equator and ecliptic, intersect in two points, opposite each other (marked by arrows on the drawing), and one half of the ecliptic (where the *Twins* are) is above, that is north of, the equator, while the other half (the *Archer* half) is south of it.

When the sun, on its yearly course along the ecliptic, reaches either of the two points of inter-

---

[1] Those of us not in possession of stratosphere balloons cannot see the constellation the sun is in, at a given moment, because the sun blots it out. But we can always tell by watching the sky at night: the constellation crossing our meridian at midnight is opposite the one the sun is in at the moment, and our model shows roughly which is opposite which.

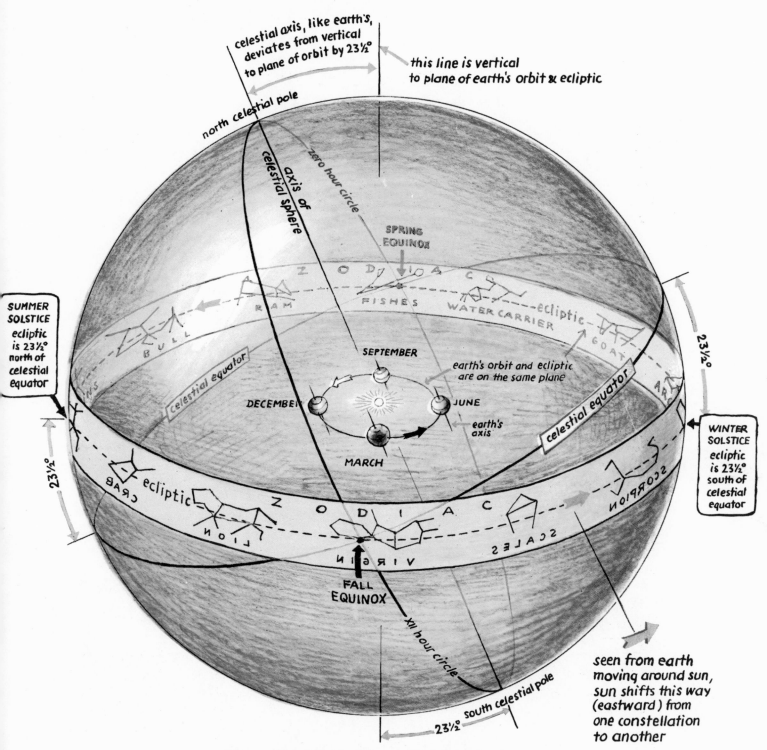

Figure 19: Earth's Orbit inside Celestial Sphere

As on all our models, proportions on this one are not drawn to scale. Sun is too small, earth too big, and sky globe much too small in relation to orbit. Pole Star on sky globe's top ought to be many miles away, so that earth's orbit, including sun, shrinks to a pinpoint in comparison with globe. The four separate axes piercing the tiny earth globes on our model would melt into one, and practically coincide with the celestial axis, as is the case in nature. Such inaccuracies are unavoidable but, once explained, become irrelevant.

section, it is, for that moment, on the equator. As we saw on page 114, stars on the celestial equator are above and below the horizon 12 hours each, and the same goes for the sun as it crosses the equator. At those points day and night are of equal length, and they are therefore called EQUINOXES (from Latin *aequus,* equal, and *nox,* night), one being the VERNAL (from Latin *ver,* spring) or SPRING EQUINOX, when the sun is in the *Fishes;* the other, the AUTUMNAL (from Latin *autumnus,* fall) or FALL EQUINOX, when the sun is in the *Virgin.* This happens on or about March 21 and September 23 and marks the beginning of spring and fall.

The rest of the year, however, night and day are not equal, and this is what happens: as the sun appears to drift eastward along the ecliptic from, say, the *Fishes* toward the *Ram,* its distance from the celestial equator (that is, its northern declination) increases, and it is longer above the horizon than below in the northern hemisphere. After one quarter of its yearly course, in the *Twins,* it reaches its greatest distance from the equator: its northern declination is 23½°: the day is longest, the night shortest. From now on, declination and day's length decrease. At the fall equinox, day and night are equal again. Thereafter the sun's declination becomes "minus," that is, southern: the sun spends more time below the horizon than above; days grow shorter, nights longer till, about December 22, the sun reaches that point of the ecliptic (in the *Archer*) which is farthest south of the equator; its declination now is —23½°. The day is now shortest, the night longest. This marks another turning point: from now on the days become longer, the nights shorter, and at the vernal equinox the yearly cycle starts again.

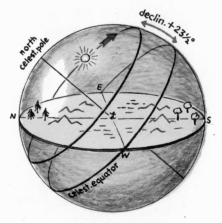 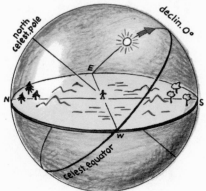 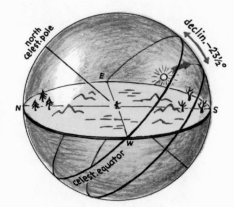

| Sun's Course on June 21 | Sun's Course March 21 and September 23 | Sun's Course December 22 |
|---|---|---|
| Sun rises NE, sets NW, above horizon about 15 h. Sun is N of Equator. | Sun rises E, sets W, above horizon 12 h. Sun is on Equator. | Sun rises SE, sets SW, above horizon about 9 h. Sun is S of Equator. |

Figure 20: Sun's Daily Course at Solstices and Equinoxes

The turning points, on or about June 21 and December 22, are called SUMMER and WINTER SOLSTICE (from Latin *sol*, sun, and *stare*, stand still), and the passing of the sun through the equinoxes and solstices marks the beginning of our four seasons.[1]

The apparent course of the sun across the sky seen from 40° north latitude on the days of solstice and both equinoxes is shown in figure 20.

How long the longest day and how short the shortest, depends on one's latitude. On the earth's equator, day and night are of even length throughout the year, but as one moves away from the equator—north or south—the seasonal differences appear and become the greater the closer one gets to the earth's poles. In our latitudes—about 40°—the longest day lasts about 15 hours, the shortest, 9 hours. Inside the polar circles, within 23½° of the poles, you have midnight sun in midsummer: the longest day lasts 24 hours and so does the longest night. And on the poles, night and day last 6 months each.

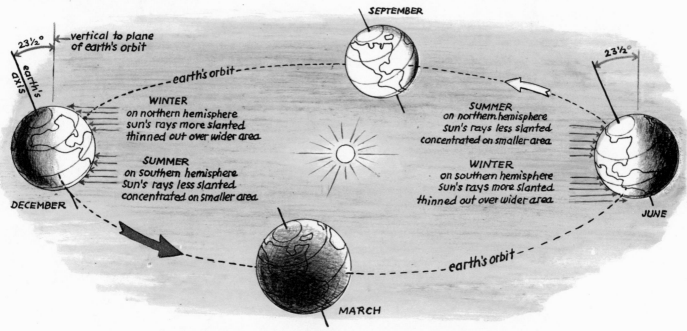

Figure 21:   Tilt of Earth's Axis Causes the Seasons

Longer days and shorter nights, and vice versa, would alone explain why summer is warm and winter cold. But another fact, also resulting from the slant of the earth's axis, makes summers even warmer and winters colder: the angle at which the sun's rays fall on the earth at the different seasons.

As figure 21 shows, the sun's rays strike the earth at a much sharper slant in winter than in summer. The same amount of sunshine is thus thinned out over a greater area in winter than in summer, and besides the rays must penetrate a greater portion of the earth's atmosphere, and this dilutes their effect even more. It is true that not June, but July and August are our hottest months, and that September is warmer than March, but it is not the sun's direct responsibility; the heat stored up daily by the earth in summer, and lost daily in winter, accounts for that.

[1] The seasons of the southern hemisphere of the earth are the opposite of ours. When we have spring, people in the Argentine have fall, and when at Washington, D.C., the sun appears for little more than 9 hours, in mid-December, people in Melbourne, Australia, a corresponding southern latitude, see it for about 15 hours.

# SOLAR AND SIDEREAL DAY

Anyone can find out, just by watching the sky, that the same stars culminate about four minutes earlier every day; in other words, that the sidereal day is about four minutes shorter than the solar day. But *observing a phenomenon* and *finding its reasons* are two things: we still have to *explain* this daily gain of four minutes which causes our skies to change through the year.

The *sidereal day,* the time between two transits of the equinox, is very nearly the time it takes the earth to make one complete turn around itself: the *time of the true rotation of the earth,* which causes the apparent rotation of the stars. We saw that on page 112.

The *solar day* is *not a measure of this true rotation.* It is, as we saw, the average time from one noon to the next; a place on earth has noon when the sun is in its meridian; when the place faces the sun, to put it graphically.

The two days, sidereal and solar, are not of the same length because the earth, while rotating around its axis, also travels around the sun. A careful look at figure 22 plus a bit of reflection shows how this comes about.

We see the earth at four different points on its way around the sun. As it travels along its orbit, it rotates around its axis. Both motions go in the same direction: from west to east. On the earth globe, our continent is sketchily outlined and a point roughly in the center of the United States—it could be Topeka, Kansas—is marked by a tiny cross.

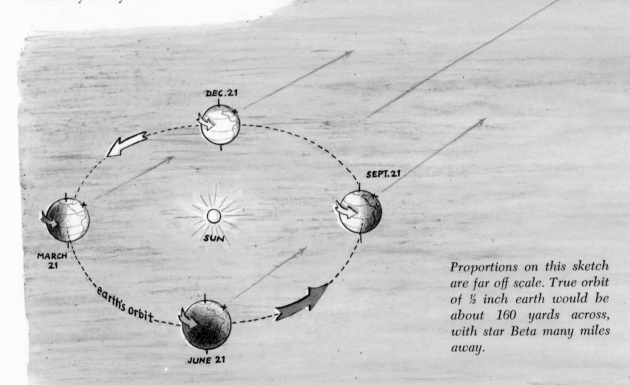

*Proportions on this sketch are far off scale. True orbit of ½ inch earth would be about 160 yards across, with star Beta many miles away.*

Figure 22:   Sun-Day and Star-Day through the Year

Let us start on March 21. The earth as shown on the drawing is turned so that Topeka is facing the sun: the sun, in other words, is in Topeka's meridian, it is noon, Topeka time. If Topekans could see the stars in daytime they would see a number of stars on, or close to, the meridian; all culminating, or nearly so, at noon March 21. Let us pick a bright one: Beta ($\beta$) in Cassiopeia, which is practically on the meridian at that moment. (If a Topekan had a rocket plane and went high up into the stratosphere he actually would see stars and sun at the same time; it has been done.)

After the earth has made one full turn around itself, Topeka will face star Beta again, but not yet the sun, because the earth has moved a stretch along its orbit meanwhile. Therefore the earth must turn a little bit farther to the left to bring Topeka exactly face to face with the sun. This additional turn is too small to be judged from the drawing but as the process repeats itself daily, the difference soon becomes striking.

To simplify our figures let us assume the year had 12 months of 30 days each: on June 21, after 90 true turns around its axis—that is, after 90 sidereal days—Topeka faces star Beta for the 90th time since we started. But now one can clearly see, even on this small sketch, that the earth must make a quarter turn to bring Topeka face to face with the sun for the 90th time. In other words, 90 solar days are not yet completed. Noon is 6 hours off, the time it will take the earth to make that quarter turn. It is 6 A.M. solar time; the star has gained 6 hours.

On September 21, after another 90 true rotations—180 sidereal days having passed in all—Topeka faces the star Beta for the 180th time, but not yet the sun. It faces in the opposite direction now, and a complete half-turn is necessary to bring the Kansan capital face to face with the sun: noon is 12 hours off. In other words, it is midnight, solar time, and the stars have gained 12 hours. On December 21, the difference is 18 hours, the earth has three-quarters of a full turn to make before it becomes noon at Topeka, and on March 21, the total gain is 24 hours—one complete rotation.

Gaining 24 hours in 360 days means gaining 2 hours a month, or exactly 4 minutes a day. Now our year has 365.24 solar days (but 366.24 sidereal days)—so the gain of 24 hours is spread over a few more days than we assumed above, and the *daily* gain, therefore, is a trifle smaller; it comes to 3 minutes 55.91 seconds a day, and this is meant when we say that "the stars gain about four minutes daily."

NOTE: We could use any star as a test star but Beta of Cassiopeia has the advantage of being practically on the zero hour circle, and you can read the sidereal time from this hour circle as though from a clock hand, any night of the year; if you have the sidereal time you can, by simple addition of four minutes a day, figure out your own solar time. It's a nice pastime and could even be useful. How to do it is shown on the next two pages.

This chart shows Cassiopeia and Big Dipper, from hour to hour, circling around Pole Star. One full circle marks one SIDEREAL DAY. White numbers below each position show the hour, SIDEREAL

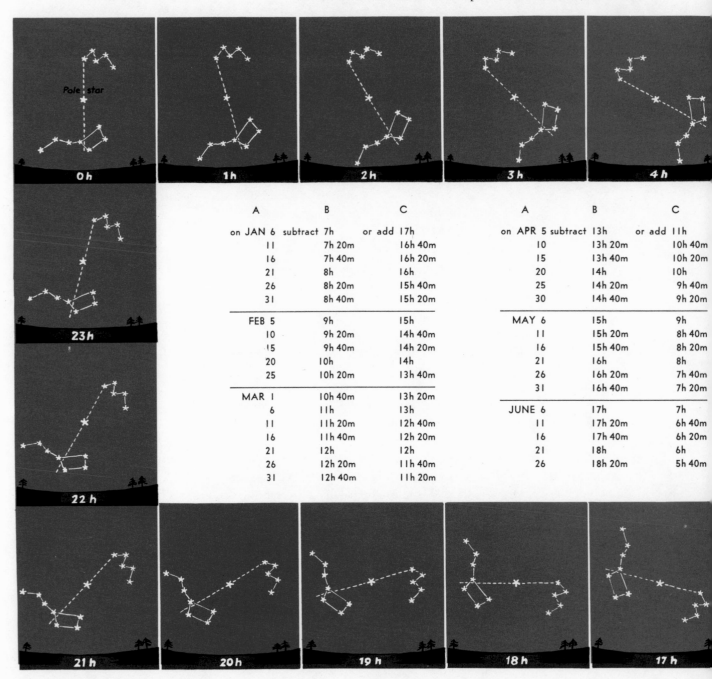

| | A | B | C | | A | B | C |
|---|---|---|---|---|---|---|---|
| on JAN 6 | subtract | 7h | or add 17h | on APR 5 | subtract | 13h | or add 11h |
| 11 | | 7h 20m | 16h 40m | 10 | | 13h 20m | 10h 40m |
| 16 | | 7h 40m | 16h 20m | 15 | | 13h 40m | 10h 20m |
| 21 | | 8h | 16h | 20 | | 14h | 10h |
| 26 | | 8h 20m | 15h 40m | 25 | | 14h 20m | 9h 40m |
| 31 | | 8h 40m | 15h 20m | 30 | | 14h 40m | 9h 20m |
| FEB 5 | | 9h | 15h | MAY 6 | | 15h | 9h |
| 10 | | 9h 20m | 14h 40m | 11 | | 15h 20m | 8h 40m |
| 15 | | 9h 40m | 14h 20m | 16 | | 15h 40m | 8h 20m |
| 20 | | 10h | 14h | 21 | | 16h | 8h |
| 25 | | 10h 20m | 13h 40m | 26 | | 16h 20m | 7h 40m |
| | | | | 31 | | 16h 40m | 7h 20m |
| MAR 1 | | 10h 40m | 13h 20m | JUNE 6 | | 17h | 7h |
| 6 | | 11h | 13h | 11 | | 17h 20m | 6h 40m |
| 11 | | 11h 20m | 12h 40m | 16 | | 17h 40m | 6h 20m |
| 16 | | 11h 40m | 12h 20m | 21 | | 18h | 6h |
| 21 | | 12h | 12h | 26 | | 18h 20m | 5h 40m |
| 26 | | 12h 20m | 11h 40m | | | | |
| 31 | | 12h 40m | 11h 20m | | | | |

Fig

HOW TO USE THIS CHART: From 24 positions shown here pick the one closest to what you see in the sky. From column A pick date closest to your date of observation. From white number underneath that position, SUBTRACT number of hours in column B, for that date, or ADD number of hours in column C, whichever is easier. If your observation date is one of those printed in column A, the result is your own SOLAR TIME. If your date is between two printed dates, you add or subtract accordingly a few minutes less or more: four minutes per day you are off. If you have daylight saving time, subtract one hour from your result. At midnight September 23 sidereal and solar time are even. Around that time, you can read the hour from the chart "as is" —no additions or subtractions (except daylight saving time).

# CELESTIAL CLOCK

TIME, at which that position is reached, any day of the year: it never changes. How to translate these hours SIDEREAL TIME into your own STANDARD (i.e., SOLAR) TIME is shown below.

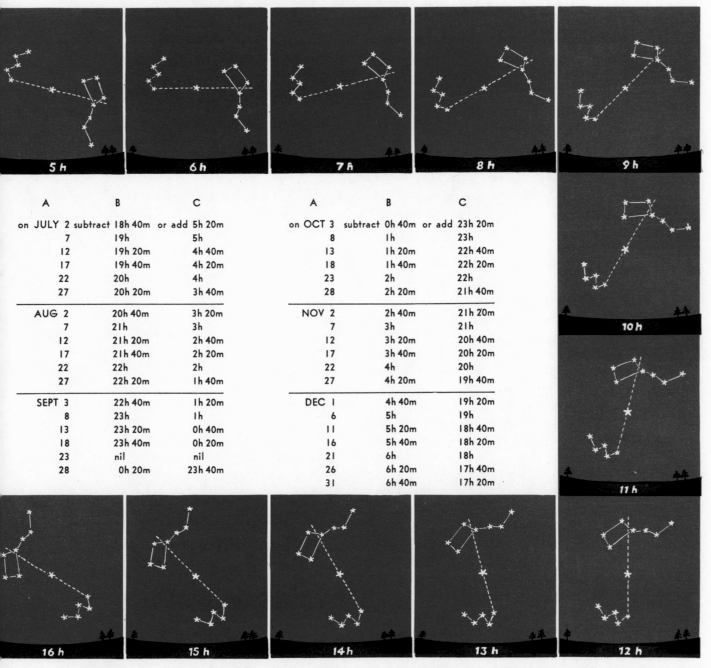

| A | B | C | | A | B | C |
|---|---|---|---|---|---|---|
| on JULY 2 subtract | 18h 40m | or add 5h 20m | | on OCT 3 subtract | 0h 40m | or add 23h 20m |
| 7 | 19h | 5h | | 8 | 1h | 23h |
| 12 | 19h 20m | 4h 40m | | 13 | 1h 20m | 22h 40m |
| 17 | 19h 40m | 4h 20m | | 18 | 1h 40m | 22h 20m |
| 22 | 20h | 4h | | 23 | 2h | 22h |
| 27 | 20h 20m | 3h 40m | | 28 | 2h 20m | 21h 40m |
| AUG 2 | 20h 40m | 3h 20m | | NOV 2 | 2h 40m | 21h 20m |
| 7 | 21h | 3h | | 7 | 3h | 21h |
| 12 | 21h 20m | 2h 40m | | 12 | 3h 20m | 20h 40m |
| 17 | 21h 40m | 2h 20m | | 17 | 3h 40m | 20h 20m |
| 22 | 22h | 2h | | 22 | 4h | 20h |
| 27 | 22h 20m | 1h 40m | | 27 | 4h 20m | 19h 40m |
| SEPT 3 | 22h 40m | 1h 20m | | DEC 1 | 4h 40m | 19h 20m |
| 8 | 23h | 1h | | 6 | 5h | 19h |
| 13 | 23h 20m | 0h 40m | | 11 | 5h 20m | 18h 40m |
| 18 | 23h 40m | 0h 20m | | 16 | 5h 40m | 18h 20m |
| 23 | nil | nil | | 21 | 6h | 18h |
| 28 | 0h 20m | 23h 40m | | 26 | 6h 20m | 17h 40m |
| | | | | 31 | 6h 40m | 17h 20m |

EXAMPLE: You see the star group in "5ʰ" position, on February 8. What time is it? Nearest date in column A: February 10. Table tells you to subtract 9ʰ20ᵐ for that date, or to add 14ʰ40ᵐ, whichever is easier, so you add 14ʰ40ᵐ. Result: 19ʰ40ᵐ (7:40 P.M.). But this is February 10 time. On February 8, you are 2 days (8 minutes) too early; your correct time is 7:48 P.M.

In practice our sky clock is not that exact. It only works approximately. Observation by instrument would be needed for precise work. But with some practice you get fair results. The point is to estimate intermediate values correctly in the tilt of the group as well as on the time table. Also, your standard time may vary from your local mean solar time if you are near the border of a time zone, by as much as 30 minutes or more. See notes on this subject on next page.

# TIME AND TIME ZONES

To the non-stargazing mortal, time is a simple affair. He reads it from his watch, which he adjusts by the clock in the railroad station or by the radio time signal. But railroads and radio stations must in turn keep their clocks right and they do this by checking with time signals given by astronomical observatories, and these check their clocks by the *stars:* the astronomers, for their observations, use

SIDEREAL TIME, i.e., Star Time, which is based on the true rotation of the earth in relation not to the sun, but to a certain point of the star sphere: the *vernal equinox* (figure 19). The interval between two successive culminations of this point constitutes the *sidereal day,* which is by now an old acquaintance of ours (see page 112).

Star time is thus the ultimate foundation upon which all our timekeeping rests, although most of us are not aware of it as we run our lives by

SOLAR TIME or Sun Time. The term Solar Time, however, is not quite definite because there are two different kinds of it: *apparent solar time* and *mean solar time.* A specific type of the latter, known by all as *standard time,* is our "everyday time." To understand what this standard time is we must first know what is meant by

APPARENT SOLAR TIME: This is the time we see when we watch a sundial. The sundial shows *noon* when the sun actually crosses the meridian, and the interval between two such successive crossings is the APPARENT SOLAR DAY (counted from midnight to midnight to avoid change of date at noon). This is an obvious and natural way of measuring time and it was good enough in ages past, but it will not do for accurate and uniform timekeeping as required in our modern world because those apparent solar days are not of even length. The sun's apparent daily motion across the sky is not even through the year.[1] It sometimes seems to move slightly faster, sometimes slightly slower, and the intervals between two successive noons are therefore not all of the same length. They vary by almost one minute, and were our clocks to go by the sun as we see it, they would have to be speeded up or slowed down all the time, according to the sun, and that would be impractical.

Besides, apparent solar time is strictly local. The apparent noon shifts with every change of longitude; for every quarter-degree of longitude (about 13 miles in our latitudes) that we move east or west, it occurs one minute earlier or later.

To overcome the first of these two inconveniences—the uneven length of the apparent solar day—astronomers have established MEAN SOLAR TIME. Its basis is the average length of the apparent solar days over the year, the MEAN SOLAR DAY.[2] Its twenty-four hours are the ones your watch is supposed to show when it is well regulated. The hours, minutes, and seconds ticked off by our clocks and watches are mean solar hours, minutes, and seconds.

[1] One reason (not the only one) is that the earth's orbit is not a perfect circle with the sun at its center but slightly elliptic with the sun at one focus. The earth therefore is sometimes nearer to, sometimes farther from, the sun. It travels faster along its orbit when nearer, and slower when farther, and accordingly the sun seems to travel across the sky at slightly varying speed. The deviation from the true circle is not great: about 3 per cent; one would hardly notice it on a drawing. When nearest the sun, in the PERIHELION (Greek *peri,* near, *helios* sun), the earth is about three million miles closer than in the APHELION (*apo,* off), its mean distance from the sun being about ninety-three million miles. Accordingly it is 186 days from spring to fall equinox, on the northern half of the globe, and 179 days from fall to spring, also about 3 per cent difference. Summer, in our hemisphere, is about a week longer than winter. In the southern hemisphere the opposite is true.

[2] It is to this mean solar day that we refer when saying that the sidereal day is $3^m55^s.91$ shorter than the solar day; solar minutes and seconds, that is. The sidereal day has twenty-four sidereal hours which are, of course, shorter by the same ratio than solar hours, and so are sidereal minutes and seconds.

But there remained the second inconvenience: the mean solar day, though unvarying in length, was still local. Noon by LOCAL CIVIL TIME, as this kind of time is called, shifts with varying longitude as does the apparent noon, by one minute per quarter-degree. Under this system larger or smaller communities all over the world each had their clocks based on Local Civil Time, and this caused endless confusion until

STANDARD TIME was internationally established. It was a slow process, beginning with an international congress in Washington in 1884 and going on over several decades. As a result, the world is now divided into twenty-four TIME ZONES, each 15° of longitude wide (with slight variations for practical reasons) and differing among each other by one hour. In each zone, time is based on the mean solar time of the central meridian of the zone. On this meridian, the *standard meridian*, standard time is identical with local civil time but as one moves toward the border of a zone, 7½° on the average, from its middle, standard time and local civil time differ by about 30 minutes; near the eastern border of a zone your watch, keeping standard time, will be about 30 minutes slow as against local civil time, and near the western border, fast: a noticeable difference if one tries to read the time from the stars as described on the preceding page but otherwise not too bothersome.

This is how matters stand with time at present and will probably remain for some time to come.

# THE PRECESSION OF THE EQUINOXES

The equinox, whose culminations define the sidereal day, does not keep its place on the star sphere. We noted this in passing on page 112. We also saw, when discussing the constellations, that Polaris was not always the pole star but that other stars have been or will be pole stars at different times due to the shift of the celestial pole: Thuban, e.g., or Vega.

Both shifts—of the equinox and of the pole—are but two aspects of one and the same phenomenon, generally known as the PRECESSION OF THE EQUINOXES. As early as 125 B.C. the Greek astronomer Hipparchus discovered it, but only eighteen centuries later Sir Isaac Newton found the explanation. What happens is this:

The celestial pole is the point in the sky to which the axis of our rotating planet points and the center around which the sky appears to rotate. If the earth were a perfect sphere, this axis would always point to the same spot. However, the earth is not a perfect sphere but is a little flattened at the poles and a little thicker at the equator, and this causes the axis to wobble the way a slowing-down top does. While the tilt of the axis to the earth's orbit remains the same (deviating 23½° from the vertical), the axis itself describes a funnel-shaped motion, once around in about 25,800 years. If we made a model of this setup, on which the prolongation of the earth's axis had a pencil point, that pencil point would describe a circle on the vault of our model sky. This circle is shown at the top of figure 24. Stars which are on or near this circle become pole stars, successively, in the course of 25,800 years. This time span—one complete wobble—is called the PLATONIC YEAR.

POLARIS is very close to this circle, and the celestial pole wandering along the circle is now only 1° away from Polaris. A few thousand years ago, within recorded history, the pole was much farther away from Polaris and much closer to the star THUBAN in the DRAGON'S tail: this was the pole star when the Pyramids were being built, during the third millennium B.C.

During the next century, the celestial pole will come even closer to Polaris but as time goes on will draw away from it. The stars GAMMA, BETA, and ALPHA in CEPHEUS are next in line, and will be pole stars in 2000, 4000, and 6000 years approximately. Not being very bright, these three stars will make a rather poor show; but in about 8000 years a star of first magnitude— DENEB, in the SWAN—will be reasonably close to the pole and perhaps our descendants will confer the honor of Pole Starship on it—though a few fainter stars will be closer to the pole at the time. About A.D. 14,000, an even more brilliant star will be a candidate: VEGA in the LYRE. About A.D. 18,000, star TAU in HERCULES will have its chance, but it is only of fourth magnitude —rather poor again—and about A.D. 23,000 Thuban will be the pole star again, and so on.

All these are rather distant events but with modern instruments the effects of the pole's wanderlust can be noticed even within a human life span. One effect is a shift, on the ecliptic, of the equinoxes. As the earth's axis wobbles, the celestial equator wobbles too (being equally distant from both celestial poles), and this causes its points of intersection with the ecliptic (which does *not* wobble) to shift from the point where they are now—in the FISHES and VIRGIN—toward WATER CARRIER and LION[1] by one third of a degree in twenty-five years—almost the apparent width of a full moon.

But the celestial poles and equinoxes are not the only thing kept on the move by the precession. Since right ascensions are reckoned from the equinox, and declinations from the equator, they, too, shift as the equator wobbles, and star atlases have to be revised and redesigned every twenty-five years; and when we said, on page 113, that a star's declination does not change, we should now say, if we want to be precise: it only changes in accordance with the precession of the equinoxes (and, being in the qualifying mood, we should add: and with the star's proper motion, a subject to be considered on page 148). Through the centuries, these changes are considerable; about 3000 B.C., for instance, the SOUTHERN CROSS, now invisible in our latitudes, would have been visible in Quebec, Canada, or Paris, France, if there had been a Quebec or Paris then.

The equinoxes and the solstices (which are shifting too, of course) mark the beginning of the seasons, so that the seasons shift, through the Platonic year, in relation to the stars. Spring, which now begins with the sun in the FISHES, a few thousand years ago began when the sun was in the RAM, which to this day is the constellation one mentions first when describing the zodiac, and

[1] Throughout the solar year (our ordinary year) the *sun travels eastward* along the ecliptic, from Fishes to Ram to Bull and so on (see figure 19, page 119); throughout the Platonic year, the *equinoxes travel westward*, from Ram to Fishes, because the wobble goes against the turn of the earth around the sun. Compare the arrows on figures 19 and 24.

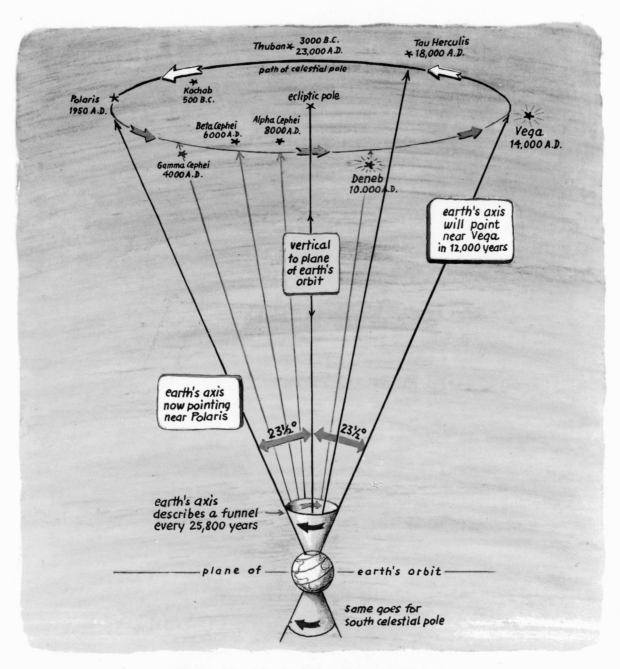

Figure 24:   The Wobble of the Earth's Axis

we still speak of the tropics of CANCER and CAPRICORN, although the solstices have now shifted to ARCHER and TWINS (see figure 19).

This does not mean that in the distant future summer will fall in December: the length of the year—365.2422 solar days—is the period between two returns of the sun to the spring equinox and the seasons therefore always keep their place in the year.  But it does mean that 12,000 years from now, with Vega as the pole star, our present summer constellations such as Archer and Scorpion —now low in the southern summer skies—will be high up in the sky in winter; our present winter stars will be summer stars by then, with the Twins low in the south, and the stargazer in the northern United States will see the Southern Cross again.

# ZODIAC AND PLANETS

We saw on page 118 that the ecliptic runs through a belt of 12 constellations called the ZODIAC (figure 19) and we also noted that within this belt the stargazer has to watch out for PLANETS.

The reason why the planets are to be found always within this belt is that their orbits around the sun are all nearly in the same plane as the earth's orbit. This goes at least for the planets with which we are concerned here—VENUS, MARS, JUPITER, and SATURN—all bright and easily visible with the naked eye,[1] and MERCURY also.

Figure 25 gives a rough idea of the arrangement, although the sizes of the planets and their distances from the sun are, of course, not true to scale. The zodiacal belt, with its unchanging constellations, forms the background across which the planets appear to be forever wandering, as seen from the earth. At the moment shown on this sketch, Mars would appear between Ram and Bull, and Saturn in the Lion; Jupiter would appear in the Scorpion but the sun is between earth and Jupiter and it would therefore be invisible, and so would Venus. Venus deviates, at most, 9° from the ecliptic, either way, and the other three even less, so that they all are to be found within a belt 18° wide, with the ecliptic running along the belt's middle like the white line on a highway. Since the moon's orbit also deviates but slightly from the earth's (about 5°), it too always travels within the zodiac and close to the ecliptic.

There are four first-magnitude stars on or near the ecliptic: Regulus, Spica, Antares, and Aldebaran. Two, or even three of them are often in the sky at the same time, and also one or two planets, and the moon. One sees all these celestial bodies on a nearly straight line (or rather: great circle line) across the sky as though lined up on a thread: this invisible thread is approximately the ecliptic; one can easily visualize it on such an occasion.

The planets all revolve around the sun the same way the earth does, from west to east, and therefore appear drifting eastward along the zodiac, with the exception of Venus which performs a shuttle course, as seen from the earth. Being between sun and earth, Venus never appears far away from the sun (the same goes for Mercury). Venus and Mercury (not on the sketch) are called INNER PLANETS; while the others, farther from the sun than the earth, are called OUTER PLANETS. The outer planets need more time than the earth to complete their trip around the sun (their Year) and the earth overtakes them at regular intervals. On our sketch, the earth is about to overtake Mars, then it will overtake Saturn, then Jupiter. When the earth overtakes one of the outer planets, the planet appears to reverse its eastward drift (called "Direct Motion") for a while and drift west, just as a car one passes on the road seems to go backward for a moment. The planet then reverses again and drifts eastward till the earth overtakes it the next time. The planet tables on pages 134–135 show this "Retrograde Motion" clearly. Whenever it occurs, the overtaken planet is opposite the sun as seen from the earth (it is "in opposition" as the term goes) and therefore, at its highest about midnight and can be seen well. For details about the planets —size, distance—see pages 132–133.

The planets puzzled mankind for a long time. Because they do not follow the general rotation of the stars but seemed to wander their own erratic paths (planet is Greek for wanderer) they were looked upon with awe and reverence. Five days of our seven-day week were named after them by the Near Eastern nations, those early pioneers of the skies (the other two were named

---

[1] The other three planets—Uranus, Neptune, and Pluto (there are eight in all, besides the earth)—can only be seen with a telescope. Pluto's orbit deviates 17° from the earth's orbit.

after Sun and Moon), and a great body of superstitions formed around them which survives as present-day astrology.[1]

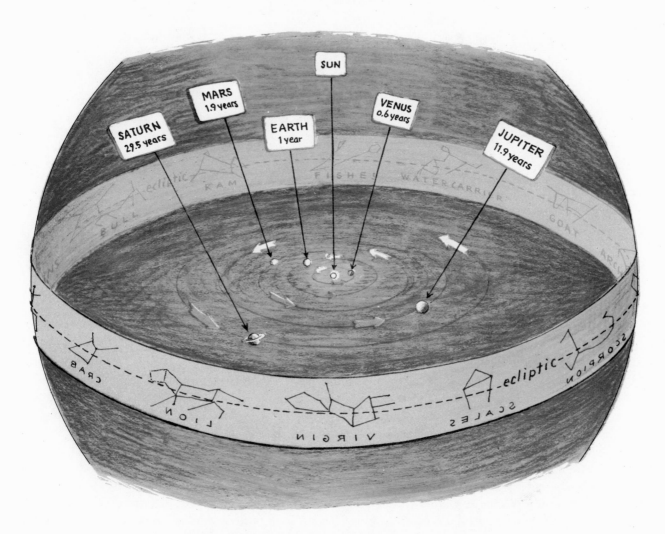

Figure 25: The Zodiac, Background of the Planets

The constellations through which the planets wandered, the constellations of the zodiac, profited by that special attention, and even today their names are familiar to many people who have no idea what the constellations themselves look like and where to find them in the sky.

In ages past, more than 4000 years ago, these 12 constellations supposedly all represented animals and the whole belt is therefore called zodiac (Greek for animal circle). Today this sounds a bit

[1] Astrology itself does not enjoy much credit today among those who think along more sober lines. Its claim to recognize direct relations between human affairs and the position of stars and planets and therefrom to predict character, fate, and the outcome of our actions is considered ill-founded and hard to prove, to say the least. Astronomy and astrology are often being confused and taken one for the other. Astronomers resent this, and rightly. Theirs is an exact science—rational analysis and explanation of nature's phenomena, checked by constant observation—and does not pretend to foretell human fortunes.

awkward as far as Virgin, Twins, Water Carrier, Archer, and Scales are concerned but the name sticks. A thirteenth constellation, the Serpent Holder, is also partly in the zodiac but for some reason, possibly superstitious, is never mentioned as zodiacal.

The 12 constellations, starting from Ram and going east, are:

| | | |
|---|---|---|
| Ram (Aries) | Lion (Leo) | Archer (Sagittarius) |
| Bull (Taurus) | Virgin (Virgo) | Goat (Capricornus) |
| Twins (Gemini) | Scales (Libra) | Water Carrier (Aquarius) |
| Crab (Cancer) | Scorpion (Scorpius) | Fishes (Pisces) |

It is useful to know these 12 constellations in their right order (the Ram is west of the Bull, the Bull west of the Twins, and so on) so when you have spotted one you can easily spot its neighbors. The following nonsense jingle could aid your memory:

The ramble twins crab liverish
Scaly scorpions are good water fish

(Ram; bl-Bull; Twins; Crab; li-Lion; ver-Virgin; scaly-Scales; Scorpion; are-Archer; good-Goat; water-Water Carrier; fish-Fishes)

This may not sound scientific but it works, and that's what counts.

★　　★　　★

On the opposite page, the NINE PLANETS are shown in their true proportions, compared with the sun—which, if shown fully on the same scale, would be the size of a beach ball, 25 inches across. Six of the planets have one or more *satellites* or *moons* circling around them. Jupiter, with 12 moons (four of them visible in an 8-power field glass—don't miss the chance), holds the record, unless you count as moons the millions of tiny moonlets which form Saturn's famous rings.

Uranus, Neptune, and Pluto, as mentioned before, are not visible to the naked eye, and the same goes for the *Asteroids*,[1] (starlets, from Latin *astrum*, star) which revolve around the sun between Mars and Jupiter. The largest of them, *Ceres*, is 480 miles in diameter, but most of them are much smaller, a mile or even less, across. Some 2000 have been spotted so far, but there are probably scores of thousands of those miniature worlds. Their origin poses a riddle: are they fragments of a shattered planet that once revolved around the sun, between Mars and Jupiter? Or nuclei of ancient comets, accumulated through the ages? Or, perhaps more likely, lumps of matter that some perturbing force kept from condensing into one single larger planet? As yet, we do not know.

Besides the planets and asteroids, one more group of celestial bodies forms part of the solar system: the *Comets*. A few of them are bright enough to be seen with the naked eye (in rare cases, a comet can be brighter than Venus, even bright enough to be seen in daylight) and their appearance is publicized in the press, so one runs no risk of missing them. Most of the comets, however, are so faint that one needs a telescope to observe them. Moreover, the orbits of comets are slanted at all angles toward the orbit of the earth; they may appear anywhere in the sky, not necessarily near the ecliptic like the planets.

[1] Only one of them, *Vesta*, can occasionally be seen with the naked eye by a skilled observer.

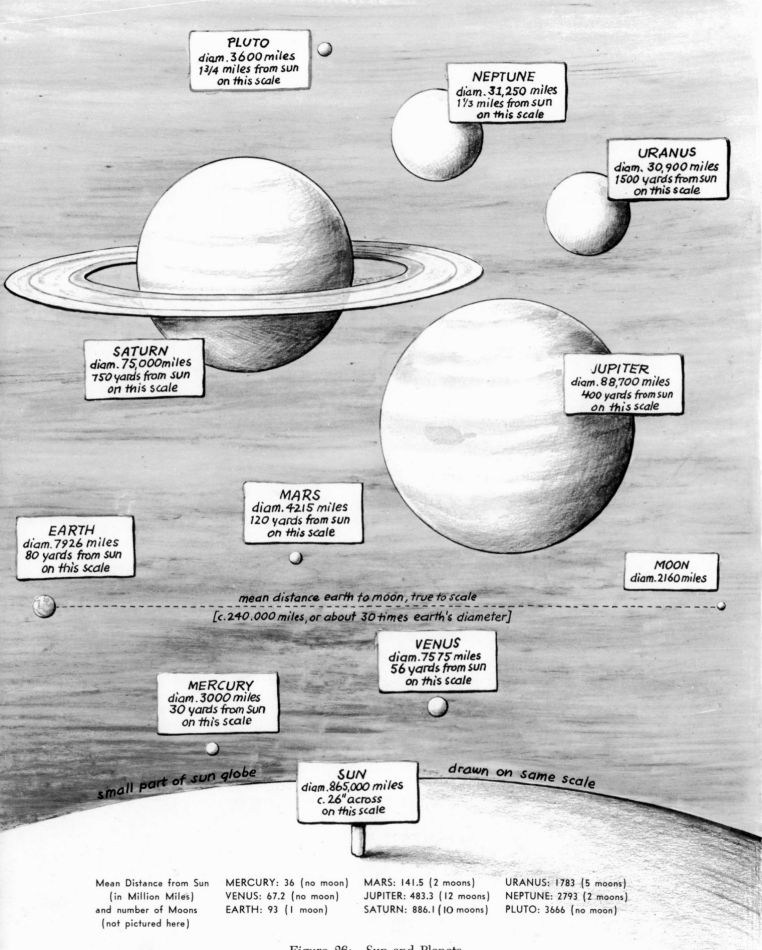

Figure 26:   Sun and Planets

133

| 1970 | VENUS | MARS | JUPITER | SATURN |
|---|---|---|---|---|
| JAN | archer O | wat.car. | virgin | ram |
| FEB | goat O | fishes | virgin | ram |
| MAR | wat.car. O | fishes | virgin | ram |
| APR | fishes E | ram | virgin | ram |
| MAY | bull E | bull | virgin | ram |
| JUN | twins E | bull-twins | virgin | ram |
| JUL | crab-lion E | twins | virgin | ram |
| AUG | lion-virg. E | crab | virgin | ram |
| SEP | virgin E | lion | virgin | ram-bull |
| OCT | scales E | lion | virg.-scal. | ram |
| NOV | scales O | virgin | scales | ram |
| DEC | scal.-virg. M | virgin | scales | ram |
| 1971 | | | | |
| JAN | scales M | scales | scales | ram |
| FEB | serp.hold. M | scorpion | scorpion | ram |
| MAR | arch.-goat M | serp.hold. | scorpion | ram |
| APR | wat.car. M | archer | scorp.-serp. | ram |
| MAY | fishes M | arch.-goat | scorpion | ram-bull |
| JUN | ram M | goat | scorpion | bull |
| JUL | bull O | goat | scorp.-scales | bull |
| AUG | crab O | goat | scales | bull |
| SEP | lion O | goat | scales-scorp. | bull |
| OCT | virgin O | goat | scorpion | bull |
| NOV | scales O | goat-wat. | scorpion | bull |
| DEC | archer E | wat.car. | serp.hold. | bull |
| 1972 | | | | |
| JAN | goat E | fishes | serp.hold. | bull |
| FEB | wat.-fishes E | fishes | archer | bull |
| MAR | fishes E | ram | archer | bull |
| APR | bull E | bull | archer | bull |
| MAY | bull-twins E | bull | archer | bull |
| JUN | twins E | twins | archer | bull |
| JUL | bull O | crab | archer | bull |
| AUG | bull-twins M | lion | archer | bull |
| SEP | twins M | lion | archer | bull |
| OCT | lion M | virgin | arch.-serp.h. | bull |
| NOV | virgin M | virgin | archer | bull |
| DEC | virg.-scales M | scales | archer | bull |

| 1973 | VENUS | MARS | JUPITER | SATURN |
|---|---|---|---|---|
| JAN | serp.hold. M | scorpion | archer | bull |
| FEB | archer O | serp.hold. | archer | bull |
| MAR | wat.car. O | archer | goat | bull |
| APR | fishes O | goat | goat | bull |
| MAY | ram O | goat | goat | bull |
| JUN | bull-twins O | wat.car. | goat | bull |
| JUL | crab E | fishes | goat | bull-twins |
| AUG | lion E | fishes | goat | twins |
| SEP | virgin E | ram | goat | twins |
| OCT | scales E | ram | goat | twins |
| NOV | scorp.-arch. E | ram-fish. | goat | twins |
| DEC | archer E | fishes | goat | twins |
| 1974 | | | | |
| JAN | goat E | ram | goat | twins |
| FEB | goat-arch. O | ram | goat-wat. | twins-bull |
| MAR | goat M | bull | wat.car. | bull-twins |
| APR | wat.car. M | bull | wat.car. | twins |
| MAY | fishes M | twins | wat.car. | twins |
| JUN | fish.-ram M | twins | wat.car. | twins |
| JUL | bull M | crab | wat.car. | twins |
| AUG | twins M | lion | wat.car. | twins |
| SEP | lion M | lion-virg. | wat.car. | twins |
| OCT | virgin O | virgin | wat.car. | twins |
| NOV | virg.-scales O | virgin | wat.car. | twins |
| DEC | serp.-scorp. O | scales | wat.car. | twins |

Check on Calendar Charts whether a constellation is visible at a given time. Watch for the *retrograde period* (see page 130). During the middle of such period the planet is in opposition to the sun and at its highest about midnight. Example: Mars, retrograde Sept. to Nov., 1973, going from Ram toward Fishes, and then into Ram again; in best position in October.) This does not apply to Venus which, being an Inner Planet, cannot be in opposition (see page 130). But one has no trouble spotting Venus because she always is much brighter than any star in the

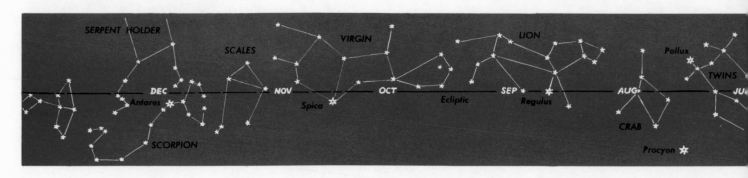

Figure 27: The Sun's Place in t

First of Each Month from 1970 to 1979

| | | VENUS | MARS | JUPITER | SATURN |
|---|---|---|---|---|---|
| 75 | JAN | archer O | serp.hold. | wat.car. | twins |
| | FEB | wat.car. E | archer | wat.-fishes | twins |
| | MAR | fishes E | arch.-goat | fishes | twins |
| | APR | ram E | goat | fishes | twins |
| | MAY | bull E | wat.car. | fishes | twins |
| | JUN | twins E | fishes | fishes | twins |
| | JUL | lion E | fish.-ram | fishes | twins |
| | AUG | lion E | ram-bull | fishes | twins-crab |
| | SEP | lion O | bull | fishes | twins-crab |
| | OCT | lion M | bull-twins | fishes | crab |
| | NOV | lion-virg. M | twins | fishes | crab |
| | DEC | virgin M | twins-bull | fishes | crab |
| 76 | JAN | scal.-scorp. M | bull | fishes | crab |
| | FEB | archer M | bull | fishes | crab |
| | MAR | goat M | bull-twins | fish.-ram | crab-twins |
| | APR | wat.-fish. M | twins | ram | twins |
| | MAY | fish.-ram O | twins-crab | ram | twins-crab |
| | JUN | bull O | crab | ram | crab |
| | JUL | twins O | lion | ram-bull | crab |
| | AUG | lion O | lion | bull | crab |
| | SEP | virgin O | virgin | bull | crab |
| | OCT | virgin E | virgin | bull | crab-lion |
| | NOV | serp.-scorp. E | scales | bull | lion-crab |
| | DEC | archer E | serp.hold. | bull-ram | lion-crab |

| | | VENUS | MARS | JUPITER | SATURN |
|---|---|---|---|---|---|
| 1977 | JAN | goat-wat. E | archer | bull-ram | lion-crab |
| | FEB | fishes E | archer | ram-bull | crab |
| | MAR | fishes E | goat | bull | crab |
| | APR | fishes O | wat.car. | bull | crab |
| | MAY | fishes M | fishes | bull | crab |
| | JUN | fishes M | fishes | bull | crab |
| | JUL | ram-bull M | ram | bull | crab-lion |
| | AUG | bull-twins M | bull | bull-twins | crab-lion |
| | SEP | crab M | bull-twins | twins | lion |
| | OCT | lion M | twins | twins | lion |
| | NOV | virgin O | crab | twins | lion |
| | DEC | scales O | crab | twins | lion |
| 1978 | JAN | archer O | crab | twins | lion |
| | FEB | wat.car. O | crab-twins | twins-bull | lion |
| | MAR | fishes O | twins | bull-twins | lion |
| | APR | fish.-ram E | twins-crab | twins | lion |
| | MAY | bull E | crab | twins | lion |
| | JUN | twins E | lion | twins | lion |
| | JUL | lion E | lion | twins | lion |
| | AUG | lion-virg. E | virgin | twins | lion |
| | SEP | virgin E | virgin | crab | lion |
| | OCT | virg.-scales E | virg.-scales | crab | lion |
| | NOV | scales O | scal.-scorp. | crab | lion |
| | DEC | scales M | serp.hold. | crab | lion |
| 1979 | JAN | scales M | archer | crab | lion |
| | FEB | scorp.-arch. M | goat | crab | lion |
| | MAR | arch.-goat M | wat.car. | crab | lion |
| | APR | wat.car. M | fishes | crab-twins | lion |
| | MAY | fishes M | fishes | crab | lion |
| | JUN | ram M | ram | crab | lion |
| | JUL | bull-twins O | bull | crab | lion |
| | AUG | crab O | bull-twins | crab-lion | lion |
| | SEP | lion O | twins | lion | lion |
| | OCT | virgin O | crab | lion | lion |
| | NOV | scales O | lion | lion | lion-virg. |
| | DEC | archer E | lion | lion | virgin |

sky. An *E* in the Venus column means Venus is an evening star, an *M*, a morning star; an *O* means she is too close to the sun to be seen well, or seen at all. If the sun is in or near the constellation where the planet happens to be, the planet is invisible because of daylight. The strip at the bottom shows where the sun is, about the first of each month, any year.

When a planet is in the Serpent Holder (as Mars in February, 1973), look for it just above the Scorpion; the Scorpion's stars are brighter, hence easier to spot, than the Serpent Holder's.

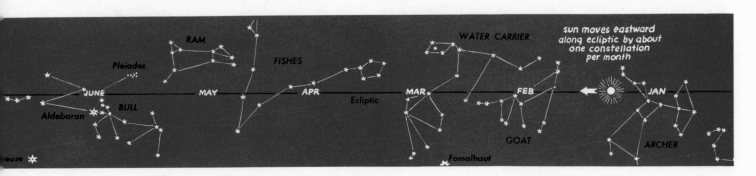

odiac about the First of Each Month

# THE MOON

In a book about the stars one cannot snub the moon, though there is no need to tell how to spot it. The most striking thing about the moon is its phases, and those who want to refresh their memory as to how and when they occur may find the following outline helpful.

Like sun and stars, the moon rises east and sets west, as an effect of the earth's rotation from west to east. But the moon also revolves around the earth from west to east and this reduces the apparent effect of the earth's own rotation. The result is that the moon appears to wander across the sky perceptibly more slowly than sun and stars, and this makes its schedule rather erratic, at first glance. Every day, it rises about 50 minutes later, on the average, than the day before and sets accordingly later too. This daily *retardation*, as this is called, brings the moon out of step with the sun and then into step again over a period of a month or, more exactly, of 29½ days.

The moon's schedule becomes less baffling if we follow it throughout one complete period, so we shall do that briefly. It is easy to do in nature, too, as the moon can be seen in bright sunlight[1] unless it is new. In fact, the moon is not just a night fixture but its appearances are evenly spread over night and day, as we shall see.

**NEW**

**NEW MOON:** When the moon is new it is between earth and sun (see figure 28) and appears in the same region of the sky where the sun is. Therefore it rises, roughly, when the sun rises, and sets when the sun does. It is strictly a day fixture then, and the only reason why we don't see it is that the sunlight falls on that side of the moon which is turned away from us. We cannot see the unlighted side because the moon has no light of its own but shines, like the planets, by reflected sunlight.

**WAXING CRESCENT**

**WAXING CRESCENT:** A few days after new moon, because of the daily retardation, the moon rises a few hours later than the sun as a narrow crescent, lighted from the right, in the forenoon. It is in the sky the rest of the day—look for it—following the sun at not too great a distance. At nightfall[2] the crescent is low in the western sky and sets a few hours after the sun, early in the night. Not very bright, the moon does not bother the stargazer much at this stage, and it vanishes soon, leaving the greater part of the night moonless.

**FIRST QUARTER**

**FIRST QUARTER:** 7 or 8 days after new, the moon does its shining half by day, half by night. It rises about 6 hours later than the sun, around noon, and climbs high during the afternoon, about half a sky away from the sun. At its highest about sunset, it shines the first half of the night. It is the familiar *half-moon* (see figure 28), though the technical expression, a bit incongruous, is *first quarter*. As the moon continues waxing, it becomes

---

[1] This fact enabled the Greek astronomer Aristarchus (*ca.* 310–250 B.C.), one of the greatest scientific geniuses of all ages, to measure the distance between earth and sun for the first time. He reasoned that, when the moon was exactly half, sun, moon, and earth stood in a right triangle. Since he knew the distance between earth and moon (which he had calculated very close to the truth) he only had to measure the angle between the lines of vision to moon and sun, to obtain the sun's distance. His reasoning was correct but he lacked the instrument to measure the angle with the necessary precision, and his result was only about one-twentieth of the true value.

[2] In this stage you often see the rest of the moon, beyond the crescent, faintly lit up. This is charmingly called "the old moon in the new moon's arms." That faint light is a reflection from the earth's light as the earth shines on the moon. The earth's light of course is nothing but reflected sunlight in the first place, so here we have sunlight "twice reflected."

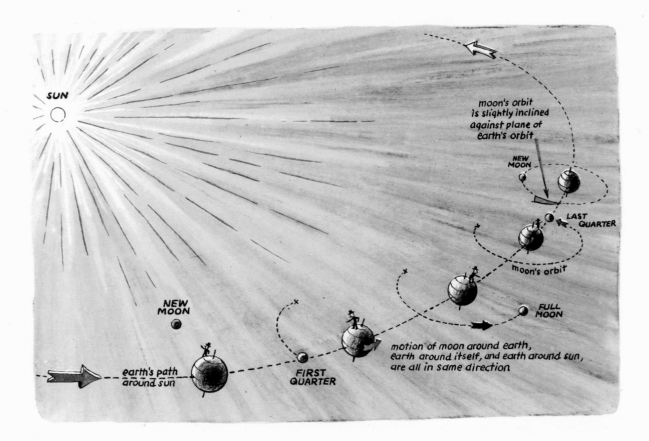

Figure 28:   The Phases of the Moon

GIBBOUS (from Latin *gibbus,* hump)—an unusual word but it is the correct term.   Rising ever  later in the afternoon, it shines well into the small hours of the morning, blotting out many stars, and when the second week since new moon is past, we have

FULL MOON: Beautiful and poetic, of course, but a nuisance to the stargazer in two ways: it is at its brightest, blotting out all but the brightest stars, and it shines all night.   Being opposite  the sun in the sky (see figure 27) it rises about sunset and sets about sunrise.

LAST QUARTER: From then on things go the other way: the moon begins to wane.   At first  gibbous, with its left side lit by the sun, it reaches its *last quarter*—half-moon again—"three weeks plus" after new moon.   It now precedes the sun of the coming day by about 6 hours, rising in the middle of the night and setting around noon, leaving the earlier part of the night to the stargazer without disturbing him.

WANING CRESCENT: Rising about 50 minutes later every night it becomes a narrow crescent  again, shaped like a C (when waxing, the crescent was like the curved part of a D)[1] but few people see it rise in those early morning hours—it shines mainly for owls, bats, and cats.   But one can watch it long enough in daytime, as it stays in the sky till the afternoon, followed by the sun ever more closely; and after four weeks plus since the last new moon, we have new moon again and the whole cycle starts afresh.

[1] One can use the shape as memory aid: the *waxing* moon, with growing strength, is D-shaped: D for *Daring.* The waning moon, feeling its strength fade, C-shaped, becomes *Coy.*

Besides giving us the spectacle of its changing phases, the moon is also responsible for the most impressive show in the sky: the ECLIPSES OF THE SUN.

The moon's orbit, like that of the planets, is slightly inclined against the orbit of the earth (see figure 28), and both orbits intersect in two points, the so-called NODES. When *new moon* occurs while the moon passes through either of the nodes, the moon for a short moment is exactly between sun and earth, causing a *Central Eclipse* of the sun.

The moon is nearly of the same apparent size as the sun—about ½°—but its orbit being slightly elliptic, its distance from the earth varies. When closest, it appears a trifle larger than the sun; when farthest, a trifle smaller. The sun's apparent size also varies (see page 126, perihelion and aphelion), so when a large moon moves in front of a small sun, the sun may be covered completely for several minutes. The eclipse is *total*, and it gets dark enough for the brightest stars to come out. If a small moon moves in front of a large sun, a narrow margin of sun appears around the black moon when it is centrally before the sun. The eclipse then is *annular* or ring-shaped. A *partial* eclipse occurs when at new moon the moon is not exactly in the node but sufficiently close, so that part of its disc hides part of the sun.

ECLIPSES OF THE MOON, on the other hand, occur when *full moon* coincides with a node. At such a moment, the earth is exactly between sun and moon, throwing its shadow on the latter. Both solar and lunar eclipses recur with regularity—as the Chaldeans found out—and can be predicted with accuracy, since all factors causing them are well known.

There are about 29 lunar eclipses and 41 solar eclipses—31 partial and 10 central—during a period of about 18 years 11 days. This period is called SAROS, Chaldean for "repetition." But, although solar eclipses occur more often, one stands a better chance of seeing lunar ones, because total solar eclipses are visible only along the relatively narrow strip on our globe where the moon's shadow falls, while a lunar eclipse is visible over the whole half of the earth which is turned toward the moon at that time.

If the moon's orbit were exactly in the same plane as the earth's, we should of course have a total solar eclipse at every new moon, and a lunar eclipse at every full moon. Present-day star-gazers would probably be delighted if this were so but our forebears felt differently: not knowing why eclipses happened, they were terribly upset by them.

An eclipse of the sun
about 19,500 B.C.

OCCULTATIONS: Traveling more slowly across the sky than the stars, for the reason we saw on page 136, the moon appears to be drifting eastward *in relation to the stars,* though its general direction is of course westward. In the process, stars in the moon's path catch up with it—or the moon falls behind—one can put it either way—and are for a while hidden by the moon. One could call it an eclipse of the star, but the term is *occultation* (Latin for hiding). Occultations occur quite often: there are several bright stars along the zone in the zodiac where the moon travels (it is never more than 5° off the ecliptic) which can thus be hidden: Aldebaran, Regulus, Spica, Antares and the Pleiades, and occasionally a planet. The spectacle, reported on paper, does not sound as arresting as it is in nature; it is well worth watching and can be enjoyed without

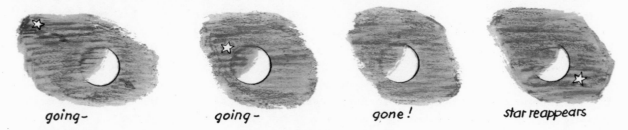

going-          going-          gone!          star reappears

Figure 29:  An Occultation

glasses. All one has to do is to keep an eye on the moon (preferably when not full or nearly so) and on one of the stars named, when it is near the moon and to the east of it.

The moon falls behind quite fast: about a full moon's width per hour, and approaches the star noticeably. It will not always hide it—the star may slip by, above or below the moon, depending on the moon's varying declination, but when it "clicks," the star seems to creep near the moon and suddenly, as it reaches the unlighted and unseen half of the satellite,[1] it disappears as though a switch were turned off, and after an hour at most, it pops up on the opposite side of the moon with the same suddenness.

MOON AND EARTH: The moon always turns the same side to the earth, as is well known. This is not the moon's doing but the earth's. At the beginning of its existence the moon supposedly rotated fast around itself, but the pull of the earth's gravity slowed that rotation down to 29½ days, exactly the same as the moon's revolution around the earth, and nobody could tell what the other side of the moon looked like till 1959, when the Russian space satellite Lunik III took the first photographs of those regions.

The moon is taking its revenge on the earth. It causes the tides of the oceans, which act as brakes on the earth's rotation and cause our days to become longer by one second every 120,000 years. It's nothing to worry about for the moment, but in a few billion years the earth will probably keep the same side turned always to the moon just as the moon does now to the earth, and our heirs, if there are any, will have something like a 700-hour day.

So much for the future. What about the present and the past? About LIFE on the moon, about the origin of its CRATERS and its SEAS, so called, and about the origin of the MOON ITSELF?

Hundreds of experts have thoroughly studied the samples of rock and dust the astronauts brought back from the moon. These samples supplied a wealth of information in many fields, but they failed to show that there is, or ever was, any kind of life on the moon—at least at that part of its surface where the samples came from. What future samplings will show we shall have to see, of course, but there is good reason to expect that they, too, will show the moon to be *totally devoid of life,* past or present.

[1] The sketch above shows the event with a *waxing* moon. With a *waning* moon the lighted half is the first to cover the star which later pops up beyond the dark half. With a full moon one misses the switch effect, but it remains an interesting sight.

As for the CRATERS and SEAS, the favored theory, supported by data from the lunar samples, now holds that these formations resulted mainly from a massive *bombardment of meteorites,* many of them of enormous size, which the moon suffered some 3.6 billion years ago. On earth the atmosphere brakes the impact of meteorites[1] but the moon lacks such protection, and any large meteorites must have come down with tremendous force, penetrating the surface and exploding underground like gigantic bombs. Such explosions, it seems, created not only most of the *craters* (some craters may be of vulcanic origin) but often generated enough heat to turn whole regions of the moon into seas of molten rock: the waterless *lunar seas.*

About the MOON'S ORIGIN there are four different theories: the *binary* theory; the *fission* theory; the *capture* theory; and the *ring* theory.

According to the *binary* theory earth and moon were formed as separate neighboring bodies from cosmic dust clouds about 4.7 billion years ago,[2] when the solar system itself came into being. The *fission* theory holds that the moon was torn off the earth, by tidal action of the sun or by centrifugal spin, at some later stage when the earth's surface was still doughy enough for such escapades. The *capture* theory assumes that the moon originated somewhere in the solar system far away from the earth but at some point came close to our planet which, with its much greater mass, "captured" it and made it its satellite. And finally, according to the *ring* theory the earth, at an early stage of its evolution, was surrounded by a ring-shaped cloud of particles (somewhat like Saturn's rings) out of which the moon coalesced. Each of these theories has its defenders and opponents, with no final answer yet in sight.

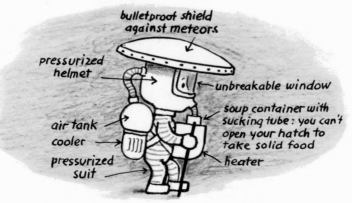

*Artist's concept of outfit for prolonged moon visit. Pre-space age (1952) but not quite outdated.*

[1] What we see as *Shooting Stars* are meteors being burnt up by the heat of friction as they rush through the earth's atmosphere. Millions hit the atmosphere daily, but only a small percentage reaches the ground; those that do are called *meteorites.* Most are small, but once in a long while enormous ones hit our planet: the famous Meteor Crater in Arizona was caused by the fall of a huge meteorite which produced a real "moon crater," three quarters of a mile across, with walls 600 feet high. A spectacular fall occurred in 1908 in the Tungus Steppes in Siberia: it devastated square miles of forest. Had the meteorite dropped on a big city, as it could have done just as well, it would have caused a major disaster.

[2] The lunar samples confirmed what had been expected: that earth and moon are of nearly the same age. But this neither proves nor disproves any of the four theories.

## STARS, LIGHT-YEARS, AND UNIVERSES

Even those among us average citizens who do not know the constellations are ahead, in one respect, of the Chaldean shepherd and other primitive stargazers, past and present: we are better informed about the nature of stars and universe.

We no longer believe the stars to be little lamps, or shiny nails attached to the sky vault, or—as one delightful Central American legend has it—the glowing ends of cigars which dead heroes are smoking in heaven.

Instead we learn at school that the stars, which make up the constellations, are in reality suns like our own—gigantic globes of hot luminous gases, some larger than our sun, others about the same size or smaller, whirling through space in every direction. Most are single—like the sun. Others—about one out of five—are doubles, so-called binaries, revolving around each other or around a common center of gravity, or even triples or multiples. A number of stars—of all types and sizes—a few hundred up to many thousands—may form smaller or larger groups, so-called clusters, traveling together through the void: one such group or cluster is the Pleiades, another is the one in Hercules (see page 38). Whether alone or in groups, they proceed through space at great speeds and at enormous distances from each other and from our solar system.

LIGHT–YEARS: Space distances are so vast that even millions of miles are impractical as a measuring rod (too many zeros), so they are usually measured in *light-years* which means not a stretch of *time* but of *space*: the distance light travels in a year. The speed of light is 186,000 miles a second, which is about eleven million miles a minute, and *six million million miles* (12 zeros) a year; so that's what a light-year amounts to, in miles. At this clip it takes the light about 8½ minutes to travel from sun to earth,[1] but from the nearest visible star, Alpha Centauri, it takes 4⅓ years at the same speed.

Distances like these are hard to conceive and even harder to visualize. If the earth's orbit around the sun shrank to the size of a dime, our neighbor Sirius would be a tiny grain of sand 3 miles away.

[1] The mean distance earth-sun is called an ASTRONOMICAL UNIT. There are 63,300 such units to the light-year, almost the same number as there are inches to the mile (63,360). It's only a coincidence but it helps visualize cosmic proportions: if the distance earth-sun shrank to one inch, Alpha Centauri would still be more than four miles away.

But only very few stars are as close to us as Sirius, or closer. Most of them are much farther away from us and from each other, and the universe we live in cannot be called crowded, though the sky on a clear night may give that impression. If we could shrink the universe on the same dime-for-earth's-orbit scale we should, on the average, have one small grain of sand suspended in every cubic mile of otherwise empty space. There is hardly a danger of collision between stars, and one may sleep quietly after having watched the sky.

DWARFS AND GIANTS: To call the stars small grains of sand as compared with the vast empty spaces does not imply that they are "grains" of equal size. They range from *giants* and *supergiants* to *dwarfs* and *subdwarfs* with the sun a respectable member of the main run; from stars with a diameter almost 3000 times that of the sun, large enough to occupy the solar system beyond the orbit of Saturn, to stars the size of our major planets, and some even smaller than the earth. We met none of the smallest stars because they are not visible to the naked eye, although they outnumber the giants and some are only a few light-years away. The surprising thing is that the smallest stars do not differ greatly in mass from the largest ones: by a factor of ten, perhaps, or a hundred at most. This means that planet-size stars are incredibly compact while the supergiants may be a thousand times thinner than air.

THE CONSTELLATIONS ARE NOT REAL: Although fantastically far away the stars are very real. Not so the constellations. They appear to us as groups of stars which belong together but this appearance does not mean that they actually do. We only see them together in certain groups from our place in the universe. Seen from Sirius or Polaris they would form different groups: we should not be able to recognize any of our constellations from there. Thus, two stars which appear to be close neighbors in our sky are not necessarily close neighbors in reality. They may or may not be, and one has to look them up in a star catalog to find out. *Castor* and *Pollux*, e.g., in the Twins, appear as close neighbors and they really are: just about a dozen light-years separate the two. But the two stars in the Dipper's handle, *Alcaid* and *Mizar* (which seem not much farther apart than Castor and Pollux), are not neighbors at all. They just happen to lie in the same field of vision as seen from the earth. Mizar is only 78 light-years away from us, but Alcaid is some 120 light-years farther out in space than that.

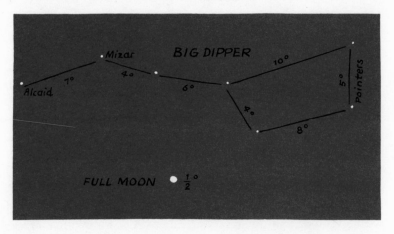

Figure 30:   Yardsticks in the Sky

142

On the other hand, *Sirius* and *Altair* (the bright star in the Eagle) are on opposite sides of the sky and seem as far apart as can be, yet they are only about 24 light-years away from each other. But our earth is in between them, and when one sets in the west the other rises in the east with the whole sky separating the two. This just proves that in astronomy, even more than elsewhere, things are not always what they seem.

To indicate the *apparent distance* between two stars—the distance we actually see—light-years are of no help. Instead, one uses *degrees* of a great circle—the same as in measuring altitudes, declinations, or right ascensions. Once around the horizon is 360°; from horizon to zenith, 90°; once across the whole sky, 180°. The stars themselves provide a few handy yardsticks: the distance between the two Pointers in the Big Dipper is 5°; the open side of the bowl, 10°; from Pole Star to the nearer one of the Pointers, 28°; Orion's Belt is 3°; the Swan, from Deneb to Albireo (the star at the tip of the bill), is 23° long; Cassiopeia's W is about 14° wide. Sun and full moon are each about ½° across. A 25-cent piece, held at arm's length (about 2 feet from your eye) is more than 2° across. You will be surprised how small the full moon looks compared with a quarter, or even a dime.

THE MILKY WAY: Besides the Circle of Animals, the Zodiac, there is in the sky another circle composed of stars: the *Milky Way.* A faint, irregular ribbon of light spanning the sky, it can be seen at most times of the year provided the night is very clear and moonless, though hardly ever in big cities with their lights and smoke. The only time it cannot be seen even when visibility is perfect, is when the Big Dipper is at its highest, and Cassiopeia low down (Cassiopeia is in the Milky Way): at those moments the Milky Way, which shifts around the sky just as the stars do, runs along the horizon and is hidden by the denser atmosphere near the ground.

Before telescopes were invented the true nature of the Milky Way or GALAXY (*gala* is Greek for milk) presented quite a riddle. To the naked eye it looks like a band of mist suggesting milk spilled over a dark table top but the telescope shows that it consists of dense clouds of individual stars. This density is an illusion, though. All those stars are light-years apart from each other but so far away from us that even the six million million miles of the light-year shrink to a pinpoint.

But why are those faint clouds of stars not scattered all over the sky? Aren't there stars every-where?[1] Why then do those star clouds form just a belt, relatively narrow, around the celestial sphere?

The reason for this is to be found in the *shape* of our universe (one must say "our" because, as we shall see, there are other such universes, ISLAND UNIVERSES as they are called): this universe of ours is a vast accumulation of stars (suns, that is) certainly scores, perhaps hundreds, of billions

[1] The sky in and near the Milky Way is richer in bright stars than the rest. Of the 20 1st-mag. stars, 15 are in or near the Milky Way, only 5 are far from it: Arcturus, Achernar, Spica, Fomalhaut, and Regulus. Of the fainter stars also there are more in the galactic region than elsewhere.

of them, arranged in the shape of an immense lentil or a flat, round loaf with a frayed edge, roughly 100,000 light-years across, 10,000 light-years thick at the center, and tapering off toward the rim. Cut in two (an odd job; only an imaginary knife can do it) and oversimplified, the loaf would look somewhat like this—

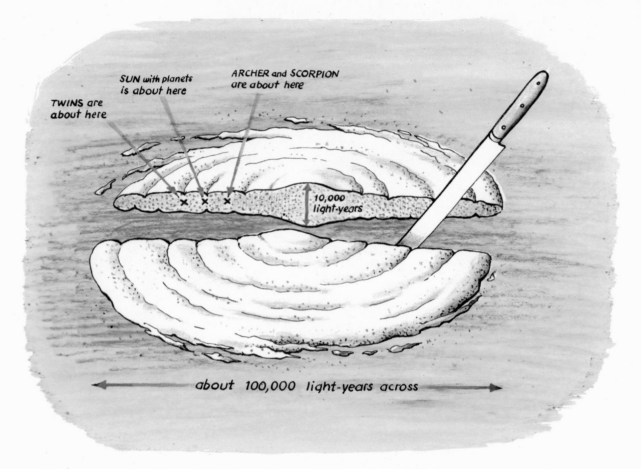

Figure 31:   Cross Section through Our Galaxy

*Sketch shows only shape, not consistency of "galactic loaf." Stars are not densely packed as this picture would give the impression but light-years apart as described on page 141. Neither has the loaf a "crust": stars just peter out into outer space which is many times emptier than our "uncrowded universe." When looking toward Archer and Scorpion (which are in night sky in summer) we look toward farther edge of galaxy, through a greater number of stars than when looking toward Twins (up in winter)  This is why Milky Way appears brighter in summer than in winter.*

with our sun—a tiny speck of luminous dust—a little closer to the rim than to the center but about equally far away from both surfaces of the loaf.  Looking toward those surfaces from our place in the solar system we don't see nearly as many stars as when we look toward the *rim*, where they seem to accumulate, and there you have the MILKY WAY: the Rim of our Island Universe.

All the stars that make up our constellations and that we can see with the naked eye, and also, with few exceptions, all stars we can see or photograph with our telescopes, are *within* our galaxy. And while all those stars, a hundred billion or more, are whirling about inside this galactic system of ours, the whole vast system itself slowly rotates around its axis, once every two hundred million years. Yet this is only a small part of the story.

THE NEBULAE: Besides the cloudy band of the Milky Way there are in the sky small isolated nebulous patches. A few of them are visible without glasses, but mostly they are revealed only by telescopes. Such a patch is called a NEBULA (Latin for mist), and there are two kinds of them which have nothing in common but name and misty appearance.

One kind are vast clouds of luminous gases floating around in space either by themselves or surrounding a star like a transparent envelope. They may be thousands of light-years away yet they are all *within* our galaxy, and are therefore called GALACTIC NEBULAE.

The other kind is more interesting, or more dramatic if you like: the EXTRAGALACTIC NEBULAE (i.e., nebulae *outside* our galaxy). Long suspected of being not mere clouds of gas but, rather, vast accumulations of stars, far away in outer space, they proved to be just that: these tiny blobs of faintest light are indeed *island universes*, galaxies like the one our solar system is part of, millions of light-years away from our galaxy and from each other.

The famous *Andromeda Nebula* (see page 40) is such a neighbor galaxy of ours, about 2.7 million light-years away. On clear nights one can see it without glasses: the most distant object the human eye can see unaided. The most powerful telescopes reveal its structure as similar to that of our own Milky Way, and even show a few individual stars within that island universe.

And those universes do not come in skimpy numbers either: the 200″ telescope of Mount Palomar, reaching at least five billion light-years[1] out into space, shows hundreds of millions of them, each containing billions of suns; some of them accompanied by smaller galaxies as though by satellites, forming super-galaxies; super-galaxies separated from each other by millions of light-years of space empty beyond imagination, each system wheeling slowly around its axis in hundreds of millions of years—such is the Greater Universe. If you stop to think it through it may well take your breath away.

[1] Some of the much discussed QUASARS (short for "quasi-stellar radio sources"), recently discovered by radio telescope, and pinpointed on photographic plates by the 200″ reflector at Mount Palomar, may actually be galaxies-in-the-making, as much as ten billion light-years away. If this turns out to be true it would mean that we are looking ten billion years into the past; when the light from such a nascent galaxy began its ten-billion-year trip to our corner of the Greater Universe, our solar system — perhaps five billion years old — was yet unborn.

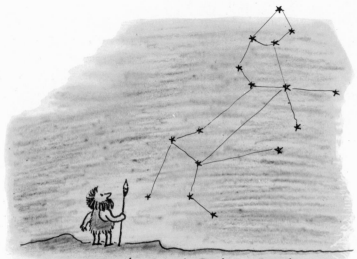

Mankind's oldest Picture Book

# THE CONSTELLATIONS THROUGH THE AGES

Returning to our constellations after an excursion into the great universe feels like walking into our own backyard after a flight across the continent, and when we consider that the very light that reaches our eyes even now as we look at the Andromeda Nebula left that neighbor galaxy almost three million years ago (by then primitive man had not yet begun to chip the first crude tools from stone) it sounds like an anticlimax to call the constellations old.

Yet what we call history—the time from the earliest man-made records up to the present—covers only the last 6000 years or so, and on this scale the constellations are old indeed. We do not know who first visualized certain groups of stars as shapes of men or beasts and thus "invented" the constellations. In any case, when *Egyptians, Sumerians,* and *Chaldeans* entered history they already had many of our present-day constellations, and we can safely assume that they go far back into prehistoric times. The constellations have been called mankind's oldest picture book, and they certainly are among the oldest elements of our civilization.

It seems that by 2000 B.C. most of the main constellation figures had been developed, and the *Greeks,* entering the picture about a millennium later, took them over from their neighbors in the Near East without changing them much,[1] and later handed them to the Romans. Hence the con-

---

[1] This does not mean that they did not contribute their share to mankind's knowledge of the skies. On the contrary, they were the first to take what we would call a truly scientific attitude. Egyptians and Mesopotamians had been excellent observers and faithful recorders, but the question why things appeared the way they did, does not seem to have bothered them much—they accepted vague, mythological traditions and let it go at that.

The Greeks pried into the unseen causes of what everybody saw and took for granted, and were not satisfied with unprovable myths. To PYTHAGORAS (*ca.* 530 B.C.) the earth was no longer a *disc* with the sky vault sitting on it, but a *globe* suspended in the void; ARCHYTAS, around 400 B.C., calculated the *size* of this globe and was not too far off; PHILOLAUS, a disciple of Pythagoras, taught that the *globe rotated,* and that the motion of the stars, only apparent, was caused thereby, and ARISTARCHUS (see page 136) anticipated Copernicus, Galileo, and Kepler by almost 2000 years when he declared that *earth and planets revolved around the sun*—a fiery globe many times larger than the earth—and that the stars were so far away that by comparison the earth's orbit was only a point. It is true that his contemporaries were unable to follow his ideas but at least he was not burnt at the stake as Giordano Bruno was, in 1600 A.D., for teaching the same theories.

stellation names, denoting heroes, mythical characters, animals, and objects, are either Greek or Latin. During the Middle Ages, when European science underwent an eclipse, the *Arabs* preserved the astronomical heritage—many of the individual stars still bear Arabic names: *Aldebaran, Deneb, Altair,* etc.—and in turn passed it on to the peoples of the West, at the time of the Renaissance.

Up to the fifteenth century only the northern hemisphere of the globe was well known to the peoples of Europe and western Asia, and the constellations known till then covered the sky only as far as it was visible from the northern half of the earth. They are called the ORIGINAL CON-STELLATIONS, 48 in number. With the age of the Great Discoveries and world-wide navigation, the southernmost parts of the sky became known and had to be charted, and on that occasion the so-called MODERN CONSTELLATIONS were drawn up by a few individual cartographers, mainly in the southern skies; but a few minor constellations were added to the northern skies also, faint star groups that hitherto had remained nameless. Those cartographers were conscientious scientists but imagination was not their strength, and the new constellations they created are not nearly as picturesque as the old ones. They completely lack the charm of ancient folklore which most of the original constellations have; one feels tempted to call them synthetic.

However, folklore was not the business of these men but *Uranography* (*uranos* is Greek for heaven), that is, charting of the skies; and their merits in this field are undisputed. For one thing, up to their times stars without proper names had to be defined by lengthy descriptions till Bayer—one of these uranographers—in his star atlas of 1601 introduced Greek and Latin letters for each and every known star—a system still in use. Instead of saying "the bright star in Gemini, in the western foot of Pollux" the uranographer today simply says "gamma Geminorum," Geminorum being the genitive of Gemini.

The casual stargazer can know the sky without Greek letters and Latin genitives, however, and they were therefore left out in our charts. They can be found, if need be, in any star atlas or on a celestial globe.

Until quite recently the boundaries which separate one constellation from another were drawn in slightly different ways by different astronomers according to their predilections, but matters have now come to a rest. Those boundaries have been fixed, once and for all, in 1930, by the International Astronomical Union, and if they do not always permit us to tie the brightest stars of a constellation together into a satisfactory shape, there remains at least the fact that full accord has been reached, among all nations, on an important subject, and that is a comforting thought.

EVEN CONSTELLATIONS CHANGE: The aforesaid agreement, however, will have to come up for revision once in a while, not because of man's unsteady character but because the constellations like everything else are subject to change. If an astronomer from the Pharaoh's court came back today he would find the Pyramids in their accustomed place but not all of the stars. *Sirius*, e.g., is now four times the width of a full moon away from the spot where he used to find it—in relation to the rest of the stars—and *Arcturus* has shifted about twice as much.

This would be quite a shock to him, for at his time the constellations were thought of as being eternal, but to us it is only what we should expect. If the stars within our galaxy are rushing through space in all directions and at speeds of thousands of miles a minute relative to each other, this is bound to alter the arrangement of the stars in our constellations in the course of the millennia.

The surprise is rather that such changes do not come about faster, but the enormous distances of the stars explain that. Just as a train watched from the station platform whizzes by in a matter of seconds but seen from a mountaintop a few miles away seems to be inching forward, so the shift of the stars appears negligible even through centuries, at least to the casual onlooker. Exact observation with precision instruments reveals such changes even over a few years or decades, and page 149 gives an example of the long-term effect: it shows the arrangement of the Big Dipper's stars in the past, present, and future, up to 100,000 years from now.

That's a long time, to be sure, but by comparison man has been around on this globe for over a million years and has multiplied in spite of occasional spells of self-destruction, so let us hope there will be descendants of ours 3000 generations from now to admire the New Dipper as we are admiring the present one.

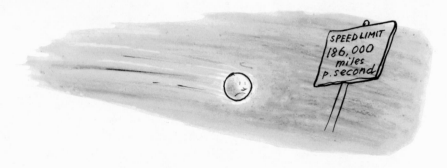

# LIFE OUTSIDE THE EARTH

When discussing the moon we found it was no likely place for life, and this brings us to one more question every stargazer is apt to ask himself, or be asked by friends: is there LIFE outside our planet, elsewhere in the solar system or in the universe? Well, let us see.

Life as we know it depends on a good many conditions. Favorable temperature, oxygen, and water are first requirements. And even if other elements or compounds could take the place of water and oxygen, some atmosphere and liquids are necessary for the kind of chemical interaction on which any imaginable life must depend.

# THE DIPPER THROUGH THE AGES

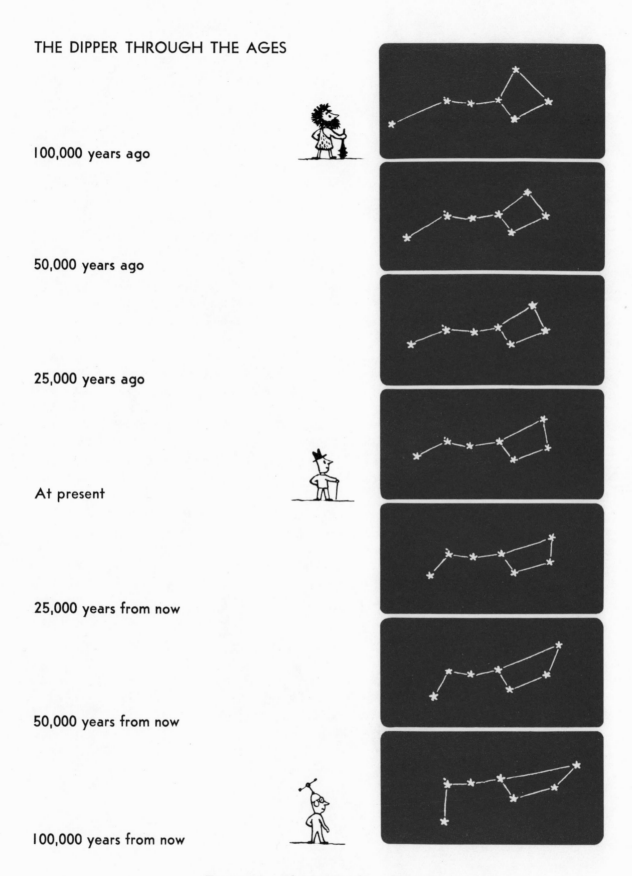

100,000 years ago

50,000 years ago

25,000 years ago

At present

25,000 years from now

50,000 years from now

100,000 years from now

Figure 32:   The Dipper through the Ages

This excludes, as carriers of life, small bodies like the moon or Mercury: they cannot hold enough atmosphere of any kind. It excludes the sun, which is much too hot, and the planets beyond Mars, which are too cold. VENUS is covered by a permanent layer of clouds too dense to permit a direct view of her surface. Some scientists think there is water, others don't, but the surface temperature, believed to be around 800°F., would be too hot for any kind of life. As for MARS, the prospects of finding life there are dim indeed. The close-up photographs transmitted by the Mariner space probes show some crater-pocked regions very much like the moon's, some featureless plains, some jumbled ridges and valleys, but no trace of a network of canals that could be the work of highly intelligent Martians. The planet's atmosphere (mainly carbon dioxide, and extremely dry) is less than 1/100 as dense as the earth's and could hardly shield complex living organisms against deadly cosmic radiation. One could argue—lacking proof to the contrary—that some very primitive life forms might endure such harsh conditions, but the seasonal color changes observed on the planet do not seem to indicate vegetation, as had been thought. However, in the long distant past— hundreds of millions of years ago—Mars may well have possessed a denser atmosphere than it does now, and may have carried some higher forms of life, traces of which we may still hope to discover. Summing up: in this solar system of ours, to the best of our knowledge to date, the earth is the only place where life exists.

And how about LIFE OUTSIDE THE SOLAR SYSTEM? Here we cannot verify planetary atmospheres since the stars, even the nearer ones, are too far away for us to observe whatever planets they may have. Yet if direct observation is impossible, scientists can build theories, and they do that with gusto and sagacity.

They rule out all visible stars: they are too hot. The question then is: do other stars have planets even if we can never hope to see them? The answer is as affirmative as such a theoretical answer can be. Planetary systems, until recently held to be a rarity, almost a freak, are now believed to be plentiful, probably billions in our galaxy alone, and new ones are coming into being all the time.

If this is so, we must assume that conditions for organic life exist on countless planets throughout the Greater Universe, and within our own galaxy as well. There may be life of a higher order, in many cases, than our own, and there is just a minute possibility that we may, one day, with our radio telescopes, pick up signals sent by intelligent beings on a planet of a neighboring star—beings more advanced than we are. We could then profit by the experience of those superior creatures.

Whether we would, if we had the chance, that is another matter. . . .

# INDEX-GLOSSARY

containing thumbnail definitions of terms used in this volume, short explanations of Greek, Latin, and Arabic names, and a simple guide to their pronunciation.

| | | | | |
|---|---|---|---|---|
| ā as in ate | ē as in eel | ī as in time | ō as in cold | ū as in use |
| ă as in cat | ĕ as in pet | ĭ as in wit | ŏ as in hot | ŏŏ as in moon |

Abbreviations: CAL.—Calendar Chart; CON.—Constellation Chart; const.—constellation; myth.—mythological character; PL.—Planetary Tables

154

# UNIVERSAL SKY CHART

The chart on the following two pages shows all 88 constellations of the entire sky. To locate a constellation look for the letter or number after its name in the list below. N (for north) and S (for south) means that you find it on the *circular* sections showing the northernmost or southernmost stars; a *number* indicates the line of right ascension (0h, 1h, 2h, etc., see page 115) on or near which you find it in the *middle* section of the chart. The constellations *Chisel, Microscope, Sextant,* and *Table Mountain,* too faint to be shown on the preceding charts, appear on this chart only.

## ALPHABETIC LIST OF THE CONSTELLATIONS IN ENGLISH

(Latin names in parentheses; for pronunciation see Index)

Altar (Ara) S
Andromeda 1h
Archer (Sagittarius) 19h
Arrow (Sagitta) 20h
Berenice's Hair
 (Coma Berenices) 13h
Big Dog
 (Canis Major) 7h
Bird of Paradise
 (Apus) S
Bull (Taurus) 4h
Cassiopeia N
Centaur (Centaurus) 14h
Cepheus N
Chameleon
 (Chamaeleon) S
Charioteer (Auriga) 5h
Chisel (Caelum) 5h
Clock (Horologium) 4h
Crab (Cancer) 9h
Crane (Grus) 22h
Crow (Corvus) 12h
Cup (Crater) 11h

Dividers (Circinus) S
Dolphin
 (Delphinus) 21h
Dove (Columba) 6h
Dragon (Draco) N
Eagle (Aquila) 20h
Easel (Pictor) S
Eridanus 3h
Fishes (Pisces) 1h
Fly (Musca) S
Flying Fish (Volans) S
Furnace (Fornax) 3h
Giraffe
 (Camelopardalis) N
Goat (Capricornus) 21h
Great Bear
 (Ursa Major) 11h
Hare (Lepus) 6h
Hercules 17h
Herdsman (Boötes) 14h
Hunting Dogs
 (Canes Venatici) 13h
Hydra 9h

Hydrus S
Indian (Indus) S
Lion (Leo) 10h
Little Dipper, Little Bear
 (Ursa Minor) N
Little Dog
 (Canis Minor) 8h
Little Fox
 (Vulpecula) 20h
Little Horse
 (Equuleus) 21h
Little Lion
 (Leo Minor) 10h
Lizard (Lacerta) 22h
Lynx 9h
Lyre (Lyra) 19h
Microscope
 (Microscopium) 21h
Net (Reticulum) S
Northern Crown
 (Corona Borealis) 16h
Octant (Octans) S
Orion 6h

Peacock (Pavo) S
Pegasus 23h
Perseus 3h
Phoenix 1h
Pump (Antlia) 10h
Ram (Aries) 2h
Scales (Libra) 15h
Scorpion (Scorpius) 16h
Sculptor 1h
Serpent Holder
 (Ophiuchus) 17h
Serpent's Head
 (Serpens Caput) 16h
Serpent's Tail
 (Serpens Cauda) 18h
Sextant (Sextans) 10h
Shield (Scutum) 19h
Ship's Compass
 (Pyxis) 8h
Ship's Keel (Carina) 7h
Ship's Sail (Vela) 9h
Ship's Stern (Puppis) 8h
Southern Cross (Crux) S

Southern Crown
 (Corona Australis) 19h
Southern Fish
 (Piscis Austrinus) 23h
Southern Triangle
 (Triangulum Australe) S
Square (Norma) 16h
Swan (Cygnus) 21h
Swordfish (Dorado) S
Table Mountain
 (Mensa) S
Telescope
 (Telescopium) 18h
Toucan (Tucana) S
Triangle
 (Triangulum) 2h
Twins (Gemini) 7h
Unicorn (Monoceros) 7h
Virgin (Virgo) 13h
Water Carrier
 (Aquarius) 22h
Whale (Cetus) 2h
Wolf (Lupus) 15h

## ALPHABETIC LIST OF THE CONSTELLATIONS IN LATIN

Andromeda
Antlia (Pump)
Apus (Bird of Paradise)
Aquarius (Water Carrier)
Aquila (Eagle)
Ara (Altar)
Aries (Ram)
Auriga (Charioteer)
Boötes (Herdsman)
Caelum (Chisel)
Camelopardalis (Giraffe)
Cancer (Crab)
Canes Venatici
 (Hunting Dogs)
Canis Major (Big Dog)
Canis Minor (Little Dog)
Capricornus (Goat)
Carina (Ship's Keel)
Cassiopeia
Centaurus (Centaur)

Cepheus
Cetus (Whale)
Chamaeleon
 (Chameleon)
Circinus (Dividers)
Columba (Dove)
Coma Berenices
 (Berenice's Hair)
Corona Australis
 (Southern Crown)
Corona Borealis
 (Northern Crown)
Corvus (Crow)
Crater (Cup)
Crux (Southern Cross)
Cygnus (Swan)
Delphinus (Dolphin)
Dorado (Swordfish)
Draco (Dragon)
Equuleus (Little Horse)

Eridanus
Fornax (Furnace)
Gemini (Twins)
Grus (Crane)
Hercules
Horologium (Clock)
Hydra
Hydrus
Indus (Indian)
Lacerta (Lizard)
Leo (Lion)
Leo Minor (Little Lion)
Lepus (Hare)
Libra (Scales)
Lupus (Wolf)
Lynx
Lyra (Lyre)
Mensa (Table Mountain)
Microscopium
 (Microscope)

Monoceros (Unicorn)
Musca (Fly)
Norma (Square)
Octans (Octant)
Ophiuchus
 (Serpent Holder)
Orion
Pavo (Peacock)
Pegasus
Perseus
Phoenix
Pictor (Easel)
Pisces (Fishes)
Piscis Austrinus
 (Southern Fish)
Puppis (Ship's Stern)
Pyxis (Ship's Compass)
Reticulum (Net)
Sagitta (Arrow)
Sagittarius (Archer)

Scorpius (Scorpion)
Sculptor
Scutum (Shield)
Serpens Caput
 (Serpent's Head)
Serpens Cauda
 (Serpent's Tail)
Sextans (Sextant)
Taurus (Bull)
Telescopium (Telescope)
Triangulum (Triangle)
Triangulum Australe
 (Southern Triangle)
Tucana (Toucan)
Ursa Major (Great Bear)
Ursa Minor (Little Bear,
 Little Dipper)
Vela (Ship's Sail)
Virgo (Virgin)
Volans (Flying Fish)
Vulpecula (Little Fox)

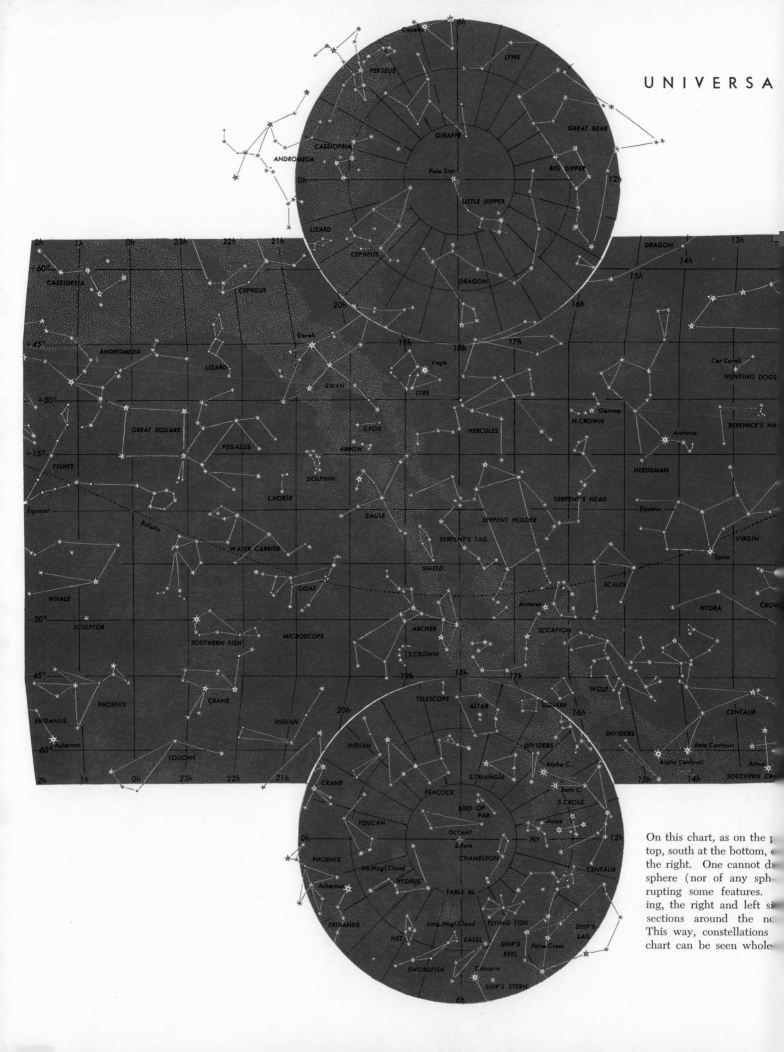

UNIVERSA

On this chart, as on the p
top, south at the bottom, e
the right. One cannot dr
sphere (nor of any sph
rupting some features.
ing, the right and left si
sections around the n
This way, constellations
chart can be seen whole

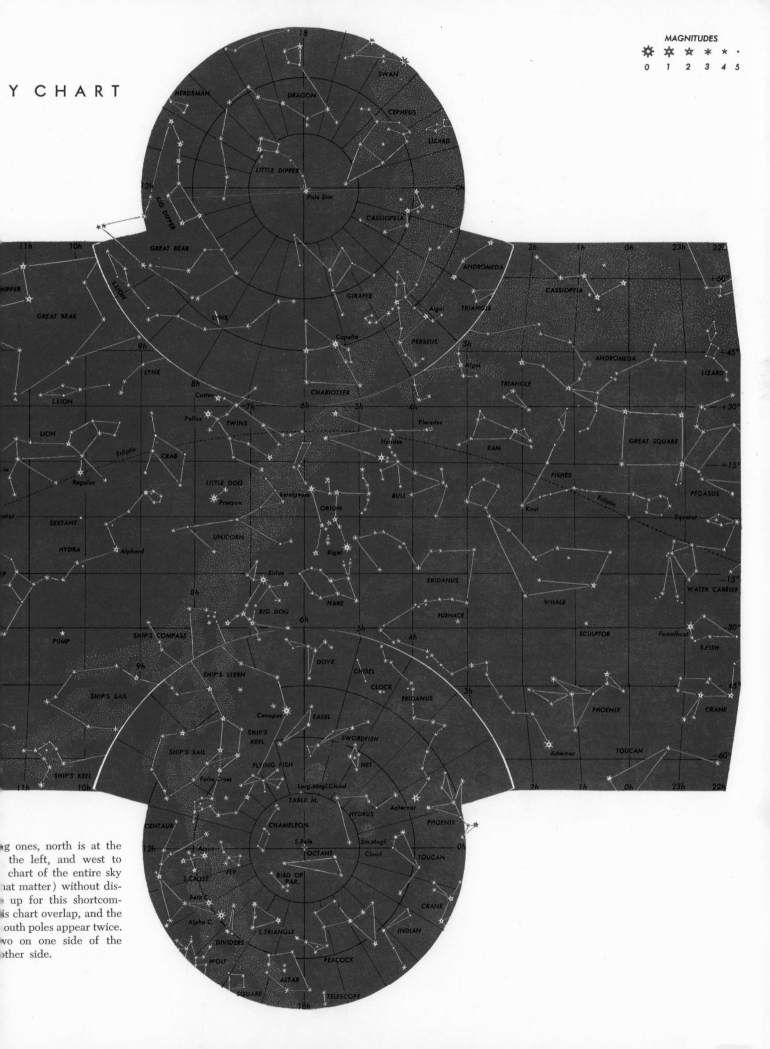

Y CHART

g ones, north is at the
the left, and west to
chart of the entire sky
hat matter) without dis-
up for this shortcom-
is chart overlap, and the
outh poles appear twice.
vo on one side of the
other side.

# THE 20 BRIGHTEST STARS

in order of brightness; the lower the figure of magnitude, the brighter the star.

*Sirius* in Big Dog; bluish; mag. minus 1.58
*Canopus* in Ship's Keel; yellowish white; mag. minus 0.86
*Alpha Centauri* in Centaur; yellow-orange; mag. 0.06
*Vega* in Lyre; bluish white; mag. 0.14
*Capella* in Charioteer; yellowish; mag. 0.21
*Arcturus* in Herdsman; orange; mag. 0.24
*Rigel* in Orion; bluish white; mag. 0.34
*Procyon* in Little Dog; yellowish white; mag. 0.48
*Achernar* in Eridanus; bluish; mag. 0.60
*Beta Centauri* in Centaur; bluish; mag. 0.86
*Altair* in Eagle; yellowish white; mag. 0.89
*Betelgeuse* in Orion; reddish; mag. 0.92
*Acrux* in Southern Cross; bluish; mag. 1.05
*Aldebaran* in Bull; orange; mag. 1.06
*Pollux* in Twins; yellowish; mag. 1.21
*Spica* in Virgin; bluish; mag. 1.21
*Antares* in Scorpion; reddish; mag. 1.22
*Fomalhaut* in Southern Fish; white; mag. 1.29
*Deneb* in Swan; white; mag. 1.33
*Regulus* in Lion; bluish white; mag. 1.34

# BIBLIOGRAPHY

There are scores of excellent books about all fields of astronomy. For those who want to study the subject further, here is a list of a few of them:

*Astronomy* by John C. Duncan (New York: Harper, 1955)
*A Field Guide to the Stars and Planets* by Donald H. Menzel (Boston: Houghton Mifflin, 1964)
*Frontiers of Astronomy* by Fred Hoyle (New York: New American Library, 1960)
*A History of Astronomy* by J. L. E. Dreyer (New York: Dover, 1953)
*Larousse Encyclopedia of Astronomy* by L. Rudaux and G. de Vaucouleurs (New York: Prometheus Press, 1959)
*New Handbook of the Heavens* by H. J. Bernhard, D. A. Bennett, and H. S. Rice (New York: New American Library, 1962)
*Norton's Star Atlas* by Arthur P. Norton and A. P. Inglis (London: Gall & Inglis, 1964)
*Star Names: Their Lore and Meaning* by R. H. Allen (New York: Dover, 1963)
*We Are Not Alone* by Walter Sullivan (New York: McGraw-Hill, 1964)

*Review of Popular Astronomy*, bi-monthly magazine (St. Louis, Mo.: Sky Map Publications)
*Sky and Telescope*, monthly magazine (Cambridge, Mass.: Sky Publishing Corporation)